More Advance Praise for
DO IT! MARKETING

"You could buy just another boring business book. Or you could buy this book. *Do It! Marketing* will help you win more attention, leads, customers, clients, revenues, profits, fame, fortune, and happiness. But only if you implement David's wealth of smart ideas waiting for you in these pages. My advice? Do it!"

—JIM KUKRAL, AUTHOR OF *ATTENTION: THIS BOOK WILL MAKE YOU MONEY*

"*Do It! Marketing* gives you the attitude, strategies, tools, and game plan to market smarter, sell more, and become more successful the moment you start implementing David's ideas. Dig into the sharply designed pages of *Do It! Marketing*, and you'll discover a smarter, faster, easier marketing approach that will unleash your business' true potential."

—JOSE PALOMINO, AUTHOR OF *VALUE PROP* AND
CEO OF VALUE PROP INTERACTIVE

"*Do It! Marketing* is a complete system for effective marketing. It is a fun read, and the ideas, tactics, strategies, and exercises it provides will set you apart from your competition."

—MARK SANBORN, AUTHOR OF *THE FRED FACTOR* AND
YOU DON'T NEED A TITLE TO BE A LEADER

"*Do It! Marketing* is for every business owner, entrepreneur, and executive who wants more focus, more momentum, more clients, and more business. As David says, 'Only action creates results.' Acting on the ideas in this book will help your business – and career – grow, and thrive."

—JEFFREY HAYZLETT, BESTSELLING AUTHOR OF
RUNNING THE GAUNTLET AND *THE MIRROR TEST*

"*Do It! Marketing* contains equal parts inspiration, information, and implementation. Do what David shows you in this book, and your business will instantly begin to attract more clients, more money, and more success."

—DR. JOE VITALE, AUTHOR OF *THE ATTRACTOR FACTOR*

"Entrepreneurs need clear, action-oriented advice on growing a business, which is exactly what David delivers in *Do It! Marketing*."

--PAMELA SLIM, ESCAPEFROMCUBICLENATION.COM

"In *Do It! Marketing*, David Newman focuses on a vital truth: It is better to get people to come to you than for you to go to them. More important, he shows you how to position yourself as a valuable resource so the market is magnetically attracted to doing business with you."

—BOB BLY, AUTHOR OF *THE COPYWRITER'S HANDBOOK*

"*Do It! Marketing* is remarkably lacking in gimmicks, manipulation, and old school marketing tricks that stopped working years ago. THIS is the missing marketing manual for your rise to the top and your lasting business success. David Newman shows you the non-boring way to dominate."

—DAVID SITEMAN GARLAND, HOST OF "THE RISE TO THE TOP" AND AUTHOR OF *SMARTER, FASTER, CHEAPER*

"Dive right into David's book, and get ready to collect terrific nuggets of golden marketing wisdom. Then, do yourself a huge favor, and take action. Apply many of them to your business, and experience some highly-profitable results."

—BOB BURG, COAUTHOR OF *THE GO-GIVER*

"Do you want to cut to the chase? Are you ready to finally make it happen for your business? *Do It! Marketing* shows you the fastest, most efficient and effective ways for you to reach higher, market smarter, and win bigger. David shares a goldmine of marketing ideas with high energy and bottom-line impact. You will absolutely benefit from this book. I guarantee it."

—DAVID ROHLANDER, CEO MENTOR AND AUTHOR OF *THE CEO CODE*

"If you're an entrepreneur, and hate marketing, this is the book you need to read. If you love marketing, you need to read it, too. David Newman has penned a highly practical, frequently provocative roadmap for anyone who wants to build their business. The book has an unyielding focus on lessons you can apply immediately, wrapped in Newman's unique, irreverent voice to keep it fun and engaging. If you're looking for some Ivy-League professor's tome trumpeting the latest marketing fad, put this book down immediately. If you're committed to capturing more customers, stop reading testimonials, and buy *Do It! Marketing* now!"

—DAVID A. FIELDS, MANAGING DIRECTOR, THE ASCENDANT CONSORTIUM AND
AUTHOR OF *THE EXECUTIVE'S GUIDE TO CONSULTANTS*

"I love this book. Your business will be energized and transformed by it. It's the action orientation that makes *Do It! Marketing* so powerful —that and the often brilliant and contrary insights that pop up everywhere. This book will get you moving, even if you think you can't move and have exhausted all possibilities. It's hard to represent in print the force of nature and wisdom that is David Newman. But this book does that better than I could have imagined. An old saw is that "It's easy when you know how." With this book, you'll begin to know how—and you'll be pushed to hard work and then ease by a master marketer and communicator. Everyone in business will benefit from this book, but it will change the lives of service business owners especially."

—MICHAEL RAY, COAUTHOR OF *CREATIVITY IN BUSINESS* AND AUTHOR OF
THE HIGHEST GOAL; PROFESSOR OF CREATIVITY AND INNOVATION AND
OF MARKETING, EMERITUS, STANFORD GRADUATE SCHOOL OF BUSINESS

DO IT!
MARKETING

DO IT!
MARKETING

77 Instant–Action
Ideas to Boost Sales,
Maximize Profits, and
Crush Your Competition

DAVID NEWMAN

Cuyahoga Falls
Library
Cuyahoga Falls, Ohio

American Management Association
New York • Atlanta • Brussels • Chicago • Mexico City • San Francisco
Shanghai • Tokyo • Toronto • Washington, D.C.

Bulk discounts available. For details visit:
www.amacombooks.org/go/specialsales
Or contact special sales:
Phone: 800-250-5308
E-mail: specialsls@amanet.org
View all the AMACOM titles at: www.amacombooks.org
American Management Association: www.amanet.org

This publication is designed to provide accurate and authoritative information in regard to the subject matter covered. It is sold with the understanding that the publisher is not engaged in rendering legal, accounting, or other professional service. If legal advice or other expert assistance is required, the services of a competent professional person should be sought.

LIBRARY OF CONGRESS CATALOGING-IN-PUBLICATION DATA
Newman, David
  DO IT! Marketing : 77 Instant-Action Ideas to Boost Sales, Maximize Profits, and Crush Your Competition / David Newman.
    pages cm
  Includes bibliographical references and index.
  ISBN-13: 978-0-8144-3286-0
  ISBN-10: 0-8144-3286-7
  1. Small business marketing. 2. Marketing--Management. 3. Marketing. I. Title.
  HV4915.N49 2013
  658.8—dc23

                                                        2012048847

About AMA
American Management Association (www.amanet.org) is a world leader in talent development, advancing the skills of individuals to drive business success. Our mission is to support the goals of individuals and organizations through a complete range of products and services, including classroom and virtual seminars, webcasts, webinars, podcasts, conferences, corporate and government solutions, business books and research. AMA's approach to improving performance combines experiential learning—learning through doing—with opportunities for ongoing professional growth at every step of one's career journey.

Printing number

10 9 8 7 6 5 4 3 2 1

CONTENTS

CONTENTS

X

PART TWELVE: TAKING ACTION

PART THIRTEEN: YOUR 21-DAY MARKETING LAUNCH PLAN

CONTENTS

XII

PROLOGUE:
DOING YOUR BEST IS NOT ENOUGH

I meet a lot of small business owners and professionals who are "doing their best."

They are working hard. Making contacts. Networking. Filling their pipeline. Collecting business cards. Phoning people. Meeting people.

And it's just not working.

Their thriving, profitable business is a highly elusive figment of their imagination, fueled by inordinate amounts of credit card debt, their retirement savings, or a spousal trust fund.

More often than not, these folks throw in the towel after a few years. No surprise that the small business death rate is a whopping 80 percent by the time businesses are five years old.

> Donald Trump said it best: **"It's not about winning or losing; it's about winning."**

Here are the top 10 reasons for entrepreneurial failure, in my experience:

1. Delivering a great product or service but being terrible at marketing and sales
2. Not getting the right kind of marketing or sales help in time—or at all!
3. Not delegating or hiring part-time help to take care of the "intelligent grunt work"
4. Not having a business plan/goal/vision/destination in mind, including the *failure to plan for failure!*

5. No differentiation—trying to market me-too, "Same-O Lame-O" boring stuff

6. Not taking themselves seriously (indicated by homemade business cards, freebie website, trying to cut every corner, etc.)

7. Overinvesting in these same things—fancy business cards, a $25,000 website, overly expensive and overly broad advertising—and thinking that's enough

8. A lack of expertise and thought leadership in their marketing focus—trying to be all things to all people

9. Failure to develop alliances (Don't think you can do it all yourself. Hire the right people to get the job done, outsource, or partner.)

10. Underestimating the time and money it takes to grow your business successfully (Remember, not all things are going to work the first time. Or the tenth. Plan for experimentation, testing, and thousands of small adjustments along the way.)

Nobody likes to throw in the towel.

But don't kid yourself by saying, "I did my best."

The real question is, **"Did you do what had to be done?"**

This book is for those who want to do what has to be done. It's not a book for dummies because you are not a dummy. It's a book for smart people, but people looking for guidance, tips, and strategies, for insight, frameworks, and basic rules for success—for people like YOU.

Ready? Here we go . . .

PART ONE

MARKETING ROCKS

INTRODUCTION

For experts and smart companies who want to stand out from the crowd...

As a **small business owner, independent professional, or thought-leading executive** who's looking to position yourself as an expert and maximize your visibility, credibility, and marketing magnetism . . .

Is this YOU?

- **You've experienced the fact** that old-school business development (random cold calling, batch-and-blast direct mail, buying ads and working hard to interrupt strangers) is broken and that **there has to be a better way.**

- **You want to win more attention from prospects** by positioning yourself as a thought-leading expert and by **executing** magnetic marketing strategies that pull (not push) qualified, targeted decision-makers into your world.

- When it comes to **positioning yourself** and your company as the experts—and **executing the daily marketing tasks** to make it happen—you feel there's **too much to do, never enough time**, and sometimes **you're not even sure where to begin.**

- **You'd like to eliminate the ups and downs of your feast-and-famine revenue cycle** with proven marketing tactics that generate consistent visibility so you become the obvious go-to choice for your target market.

- **You want to outsmart, out-position, and out-execute your competition** so that you stop "marketing by accident," and you no longer have to just settle for whatever business falls in your lap.

Small business marketing is not a mystery. It's just a series of simple decisions—and the action steps to carry out the implementation of those decisions—to help you regain the clarity, confidence, and control you need to reach higher levels of success.

Put this book down right now, and grab your FREE marketing tools, templates, and gifts waiting for you at **www.doitmarketing.com/book**. You will see references to the specific tools, worksheets, and templates you need throughout the book, so you might as well log in, bookmark the resources page, and have over 100 marketing tools at your fingertips. You'll also get the **21-Day Do It! Marketing Playbook** to create your perpetual marketing plan once you finish reading the book.

If you and your business are ready to kick some serious ass, you're in the right place. **Strap in, hang on—and let's DO IT!**

✓ 1 STOP THROWING MONEY INTO A MARKETING BLACK HOLE

A stern-looking executive stares out at you from the page in the magazine. The body of the ad reads:

> I don't know who you are.
> I don't know your company.
> I don't know your company's product.
> I don't know what your company stands for.
> I don't know your company's customers.
> I don't know your company's record.
> I don't know your company's reputation.
> Now, what was it you wanted to sell me?

This ad first ran in *BusinessWeek* in 1958. And its message is even more relevant today: You must build relationships before you sell.

If you're investing in trusted advisor marketing (it goes by several other names like **inbound marketing, thought leadership marketing**, and **content marketing**), then you've probably asked yourself, "How (and when) will this generate a sale?"

And that is the completely WRONG question to ask.

By the time you're done reading this book, you'll see exactly why—AND you'll be able to ask (and answer) much better questions to grow your business right away.

WE INTERRUPT WITH A BRIEF METAPHOR

Asking when your marketing will lead to a sale is like filling up your car's gas tank and asking, "Why aren't we there yet?"

Answer: Because filling your car with gas is a necessary but not sufficient step in getting you to your destination (a new customer or client). Marketing is just the first step, but that doesn't make it any less vital to your success. Put it this way:

Do you have a chance of arriving now that your gas tank is full? **You bet.**

Did you have a chance of getting there with your tank on empty? **No way.**

Let's drive on . . .

INSIGHT 1: YOU NEED TO SELL THE SAME WAY THAT YOU BUY.

Look at your e-mail spam or bulk e-mail folder. Yes, you. Yes, right now.

I'll wait . . .

Tap-tap-tap- tap. You're back. Excellent.

Did you see that spam e-mail from the toner cartridge company? Did you catch the pitch from the SEO firm that filled out your website's contact form? Did you respond to that great deal on vacation cruises? No?

OK. Now pop over to your paper mail pile on your desk. Did you check out the latest triple-play offer from your friendly cable company? How about that compelling cell phone offer from Verizon? *The Wall Street Journal* subscription offer? Or how about that postcard—you know, the one from the home heating oil company? No?

When's the last time you gave your credit card number to a cold caller who interrupted your family dinner? NEVER??

I'm shocked!

But you seem pretty excited about YOUR cold calls—and sending out YOUR spam, YOUR offers, YOUR postcards, YOUR sales messages.

The problem with doing it this way? In four words:

Zero. Value. For. Prospects.

And hello? YOU don't BUY this way.

What in the world makes you think your prospects DO?

Look once more at the ad at the start of the chapter and answer a few simple questions:

> **Question 1:** **What VALUE have I ADDED to my prospect's world in order to EARN the RIGHT to INVITE them to a conversation and OFFER my solutions to their problems, headaches, heartaches, and challenges?**

INSIGHT 2: REFERRALS ROCK . . . BUT THEY'RE NOT DEAF, DUMB, OR BLIND.

The next thing you're going to tell me is that you don't NEED to do any marketing because **99 percent of your business is repeat and referral business,** and it's always been that way. You don't see how any newfangled marketing is going to move the needle toward closing more sales.

Do you seriously think that referrals don't check you out online before picking up the phone? What messages are you sending to your valued referrals with:

* **Your outdated website.** Articles from three years ago are outdated, friends. And from 2005, even more so. And design aesthetic from 1998 most of all.
* **Your sporadically updated blog** that you leave dormant for two (or four or six!) months at a clip?
* **Your abandoned Twitter account** that you set up because someone said you had to? Now it has 87 followers while your competitors have 5,000 (or a whole lot more).
* **Your sketchy, bare bones LinkedIn profile** that has 200 connections but only two recommendations? (And they're from two years ago. From people with the same last name as you.)
* **Your "glory days" articles and TV clips and PR placements** from 20 (yes, I'm serious), 10, or even five years ago. Nothing screams "has-been" like old media.

Make no mistake: Getting repeat and referral business is great.

But don't kid yourself that this absolves you from having a top-notch web presence, social media platform, and body of knowledge that is ultra-current, super-relevant, and obviously abundant.

In fact, you are leaving yourself open to EMBARRASSMENT if your advocates hear back from their referrals and find themselves in the awkward position of having to defend your out-of-date marketing platform, which now casts your professional expertise into doubt.

> Question 2: Does my overall online presence REASSURE and REINFORCE the referrals I earn? Does it contain the most current, credible, and relevant marketing messages, positioning, content, resources, and value that will make my advocates LOOK BETTER—not worse—for referring me?

INSIGHT 3: TRUSTED ADVISOR MARKETING IS A FOUR-LAYER ENCHILADA.

And you don't get to eat the delicious golden-brown cheese without first layering on the meat! Here's what "four-layer" means:

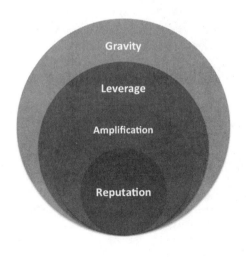

Gravity

Leverage

Amplification

Reputation

1. **The first layer—at the core of the matter—is your Reputation.** Your work. Your track record. If you stop there, you'll have a VERY hard time attracting NEW leads and prospects to your doorstep. "My work should speak for itself" is what a lot of very smart people say—smart people who have a hard time making their mortgage payments.

2. **The second layer is Amplification.** Ways to make your signal stronger. Enter social media marketing, niche PR, article marketing, blogging, keyword research, and search engine optimization. This is the key to spreading your ideas and broadcasting your expertise.

3. **The third layer is Leverage.** This is where you begin to capitalize on your trusted advisor assets such as articles, blogs, videos, podcasts, interviews, white papers, special reports, book excerpts, and other value-first marketing tools. You can now reach out to high-probability prospects both individually (on LinkedIn, for example) and collectively (on your blog, for example). This is where your job becomes putting the right bait on the right hooks in the right lakes to catch the right fish.

4. **The fourth layer is Gravity.** This is like Jim Collins's flywheel concept in *Good to Great*: It takes a long time to get it spinning but then is very hard to stop because of the power of momentum. This is where you start to see payoffs: more leads, better prospects, bigger opportunities, more conversations, higher profile alliances, more invitations to speak, publish, guest post, contribute and teach, and [drum roll, please] more invitations to do great work at premium fees for great clients who NOW know you, like you, and trust you enough to hand over five- and six-figure checks because **their level of confidence in your expertise is pretty close to 100 percent.**

Question 3: Do you want to make more sales to strangers? (Good luck with that). Or do you really want more people to recognize, respect, and request YOU by name when they have a need, project, or problem that they instantly see has "your name written all over it"? If that's your goal, then trusted advisor marketing is for you.

Reread the ad at the beginning of the chapter, and let's do a twenty-first-century spin on it together.

✳ *I don't know who you are.*

✳ *I don't read your blog. I don't subscribe to your newsletter.*

✳ *I don't see your name in my industry's publications.*

✳ *I don't hear my peers spreading your ideas.*

✳ *I don't come across your content in Google searches.*

✳ *I don't connect your solutions to my problems.*

✳ *I don't feel the gravity of your credibility or credentials.*

✳ *I don't have any tangible way to gauge your expertise or experience.*

✳ *Now—what was it you wanted to sell me?*

So here's the ultimate (and most important) question for YOU:

How can you realistically expect to SELL anything WITHOUT first setting the necessary preconditions for ANY sale with trusted advisor marketing?

The answer is as simple as it is obvious: You can't. Just like you can't drive your car from Denver to Sheboygan if you haven't first filled up your gas tank.

Only then can you get behind the wheel, plan your route, use your GPS, add more fuel along the way (and probably some beef jerky and Sno-Balls and root beer), AND put in the hours and the miles to get you to your destination.

Nobody—and I mean N-O-B-O-D-Y—hires vendors, suppliers, or professional services firms sight unseen. You wouldn't. I wouldn't either.

And the facts prove that today's buyers are just like YOU and ME. The kind of marketing we'll explore together in this book—trusted advisor marketing—is a marathon, not a sprint. And, as any marathoner will tell you, the best (and only) way to run a marathon is one mile at a time.

On your mark ... get set ... **GO!**

2 DETERMINE WHO, THEN WHY—AND YOUR WHAT COMES LAST

✴ What should be my company name?

✴ What's the best headline for this web page?

✴ What are the right words for our telemarketing scripts?

✴ What do I say to people when they ask me, "So what do you do?"

✴ What tagline will attract the right prospects and customers?

✴ What should I say in this sales letter?

"What—What—What?" needs to become "Wait—Wait—Wait!"

You're wasting your time. Truly.

"What?" is the wrong question.

More specifically, it's the **wrong FIRST question** when it comes to your marketing.

Let's boil this down to a very simple exercise. Imagine for a moment that I ask you to take out a piece of paper to write a letter.

You do so, and, with pen in hand, you find yourself staring at a blank sheet of paper. In the upper left corner, you write the word, "Dear," and then you're stuck.

Before you can get any further in your task, you need to ask me TO WHOM should the letter be addressed. The President of the United States? Your cousin Marvin in New Orleans? Your old high school sweetheart?

It makes a difference, doesn't it?

The assignment gets more interesting when I tell you that the letter is intended for your Aunt Sally. (Humor me, and pretend you do indeed have a dear old Aunt Sally!)

So you fill in the top of your letter with "Dear Aunt Sally." So far, so good.

Your next question might be WHY are you writing to your Aunt Sally? Is it to check on her health? To ask for her delicious apple pie recipe from last

Thanksgiving? Or to thank her for those snappy Argyle socks she got you for Christmas?

Let's say it's to ask for her family secret apple pie recipe.

Having answered the WHO and the WHY questions, you would most likely get busy and create a compelling, fast, easy letter with no further questions.

Notice all the things you would NOT need to worry about:

* What do I say?
* How do I say it?
* What words should I use?
* What words should I avoid?
* Will she like the letter?
* Will she act on the letter?
* Fret, fret, fret ...
* Worry, worry, worry ...

You're just going to write the letter, get the recipe, and have a great relationship with your dear old Aunt Sally. And the reason will be that **you connected with her with enthusiasm and authenticity for a specific purpose that made her feel valued, special, and important to you.**

Have you connected all the dots yet? This is how MARKETING is supposed to work too.

Figure out WHOM you're talking to, TALK to them for a GOOD, SPECIFIC, RELEVANT reason, understanding who they are and what's important to THEM. Just do that, and you'll have all the professional copywriters and ad agencies beat in no time flat.

PART TWO

IT'S ABOUT THEM, REALLY

3 WHO ARE YOU?

This part of the book is titled "It's About Them,

Really." So why is the first chapter called "Who Are You?" Because all leadership is self-leadership. All knowledge is self-knowledge.

Ha! Gotcha—THAT was philosophical mumbo jumbo. You can never be too careful reading these business books. Stay alert!

For you to be as successful as you deserve to be in your business—for you to be able to help THEM, support THEM, sell to THEM—you need to know what YOU want first. You need to know who you are, where you're going, and how you'll get there.

First, think through and make some decisions about your **business model, your revenue model, and your delivery model.**

Once you nail that down, you'll be able to focus your expertise and lay out all your possible offerings.

This is a thinking, writing, and strategizing exercise.

Allow between two and three hours for this work. It may take less time if you've already decided on some of these things, but it should not take more.

Turn off e-mail. Turn off the phone. Concentrate for 30–60 minute chunks on these questions and on capturing your answers.

Don't feel you have to write long responses; often key words or short phrases are fine. This work is internally focused, so approach it in the manner that is the most helpful to YOU.

Here's how to begin.

Take some time to answer the questions, or just jot down some detailed notes for further thought. Complete this exercise now, and you'll gain clarity on those BIG questions, and you'll be ready to make good decisions about the future direction of your marketing—and your business.

Here are the questions:

Business Model

Are you building:

* An organization (employees, sales force, offices, etc.)?
* A practice (solo professional, no employees, work from home, etc.)?
* A project-based consultancy (a loose affiliation of people and resources)?
* Something that isn't any of these? Jot down your ideas.

Revenue Model

How will you make money?
How much and from what sources?

Do you want active income?

* Selling products
* Selling services
* Selling expertise
* Short-term projects (less than 1 month)
* Medium-term projects (1-3 months)
* Long-term projects (3 months to 1 year or more)

Do you want passive income?

* Memberships
* Information products (e-books, audios, videos, online resources)
* Affiliate programs
* Referral fees
* Licensing
* What else?

Delivery Model

How will you deliver your products, services, and value to your end customer?

Do you want to focus by geography?

* Local
* Regional
* National
* International

15

Do you want to focus by method?
- 🟆 In-person
- 🟆 Virtual (e-mail, phone, web)
- 🟆 Retail
- 🟆 Wholesale
- 🟆 Franchisees
- 🟆 Dealers
- 🟆 Distributors
- 🟆 Independent reps

Do you want to focus on certain markets?
- 🟆 Business to business
- 🟆 Business to consumer
- 🟆 Industry-specific
- 🟆 Size-specific (by annual revenue, number of employees, number of locations)

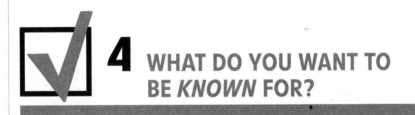

4 WHAT DO YOU WANT TO BE *KNOWN* FOR?

You must answer this key question in order to build

a solid foundation on which your business will operate, distinguish itself, and thrive.

Consider the following companies and brands, and fill in the blanks to answer the question, "What are they KNOWN for?"

Hint: Your answer will usually be a single word or concept that pops into your mind. (And the chances are 99 and 44/100ths percent that you have the right answer!)

Wal-Mart: _____

Volvo: _____

Domino's Pizza: _____

Staples: _____

Apple: _____

BMW: _____

Obviously, these large corporations had a much bigger budget and a much longer time frame to establish their position in the marketplace.

You have neither billions of dollars nor decades of time at your disposal. So, for you, this next exercise is even MORE important.

You need to QUICKLY and CLEARLY establish a foothold in your target market, build your message with relentless consistency, and deliver on your promises.

But how do you decide what you'd like to be known for?

And how do you start to build your visibility and credibility so that the folks you want to reach as prospects, customers, and clients actually have the chance to buy your stuff?

The answer: You need to establish your Thought Leadership Platform. At its basic level, this is simply the collection of concepts, methods, sound bites, and guiding principles by which you deliver your products and services. Another way to look at it is as your operational philosophy.

FIVE KEYS TO DEVELOPING YOUR THOUGHT LEADERSHIP PLATFORM

1. **Go with what you know.** Look to your own education, background, experience, passions, or specialized skills.

2. **Tie it into a common problem, evergreen challenge, or growing trend.** For example, helping your business clients improve sales is always strong; helping them improve performance and productivity is always strong. Avoid fads or nontransferable expertise.

3. **Figure out what your prospects are ALREADY buying, and position your solutions in that same category.** What are they currently investing money in that they think or hope will solve the same problem as your product or service?

For example, a web design firm might specialize in an industry that's accustomed (or addicted) to *Yellow Pages* advertising because "you've always bought an ad." Don't make your prospects wrong; show them how a revamped website is "just like a *Yellow Pages* ad except it lives on the web and it's even better at capturing leads and converting them to sales."

4. **Market-test your new messages, principles, and angles informally** with your business friends, employees, partners, and trusted advisors. Does your new Thought Leadership Platform make sense to them? Do they like it? Does it reflect the current reality of how you do business?

For example, when I started our thought leadership marketing advisory firm, I didn't want us to bill by the hour. One of our principles was, "Unlike many other firms, we are committed to getting you to your destination, not in running the meter!" One of our sound bites from those early days was "Fixed fees. No surprises. Just results." When I tested both those lines with the folks I trust, their faces lit up, and they immediately got it. You could see it in their body language. That's the kind of reaction YOU want when you test yours!

5. **Call or meet with some actual buyers,** and get their reaction *(your industry contacts, clients, former clients, prospects).* And no, this is not a sales gimmick. You really ARE simply running some new ideas by them.

If you're not comfortable taking this approach because it sounds too much like asking for a favor (gasp!), then try this reversal technique: Tell them you have some new ideas, and you'd like their help in "shooting some holes in them to see what I've missed." People love tearing down ideas (sad but true).

The only thing you're not telling them is that in the process of shooting all those holes in your Thought Leadership Platform, they are actually helping you to make it bulletproof!

In the previous sections, you focused on identify-ing your business, revenue, and delivery models. You also spent some time developing your initial Thought Leadership Platform.

Let's connect the dots between who you are (and what you do) and the tribe of people (buyers, customers, clients, audiences) whom you wish to serve. This is called *buyer persona marketing*.

But before you dig in—there's a dangerous assumption you need to address.

Buyer persona marketing is **not** about knowing your customers or what they like to buy. It's much more than that. It's about getting inside their heads to deeply understand their emotional drives.

Many of my thought leadership marketing clients claim to know their customers, yet they **haven't really tapped into the full depth and power** of buyer persona marketing.

Once you finish this section, you'll have the five keys to owning your own pair of X-ray goggles. You will be able to connect on a much deeper level with your best prospects so that you can sell more, sell more easily, and sell more often.

Hard truth: You'll be stuck in the marketing minor leagues until you realize that, to know your customer, you must first create an archetypical buyer. (Do I get an extra quarter for using that fancy word? Didn't think so.)

The process is easier than it sounds. Your starting point will be to gather as much information as you can about your clients, customers, and prospects. And don't forget to use what you've already learned from the dozens (or, more likely, hundreds) of previous conversations you've had with the folks who bought—and, perhaps more importantly, with the folks who didn't buy.

You're after the whole person: intellectual, emotional, physical, psychological. Once you begin to understand the psychological motiva-tions and emotional triggers that compel your customers to buy a certain product or service, you can much more effectively market to them in a way that will put you miles ahead of your competition.

Understanding your buyers is a bit like taking apart a mechanical apparatus to see what makes it tick.

First, you need to know what problems your buyers are experiencing every day and how they prioritize their time, energy, and money around solutions to these problems.

Your product or service needs to offer an emotional relief from one or more of these problems. In short, the buyer needs to NEED what you offer from an **emotional** standpoint and will then justify the purchase **rationally** after the fact. (Humans are capable of rationalizing just about any behavior if it triggers an emotional reward!)

Second, work to identify the rewards your customers gain from purchasing your product. This ties back into the emotional reward, but try to understand exactly what your buyer gains, on a very basic level, from your product. This will help you market to that reward and close your prospect's emotional gap.

Just as you consider their rewards, also consider, from the customer standpoint, their perceived barriers to success or obstacles to reaching that reward.

You need to understand the thought process that your customer uses to **justify the emotional response either to buy or not to buy** from you.

When you begin to build a model to break down these barriers, your product or service has a much better chance to sell itself with little to no resistance from your customer.

Third, it is crucial to understand the buying process that your typical customer uses. You need to better understand **each step** of their emotional and rational justification for getting your product or service into their lives.

For example, **do they compare other products to yours** in an effort to sort out which one will offer the best reward? If so, you need to understand the alternatives they are comparing yours to. It is important to align your marketing outputs to their inputs for vetting information, along with building an emotional connection to the problem your product is solving for them on a day-to-day basis.

This leads to your fourth key: your competitive analysis. This boils down to a simple answer to a simple question: Exactly how does your product compare against others from the standpoint of **the criteria that your customers develop to help them make a decision**?

The fifth key consists of personal conversations. The fastest, easiest, and most enjoyable way to figure out all of this is to ENGAGE your customer base in face-to-face, real-time dialogue.

Yes, I'm talking about personal conversations, either voice-to-voice on the phone or face-to-face in person.

Think about sitting down—at least monthly—with your best customers or new prospects over breakfasts, lunches, coffees. Can't make it in person? Use the phone or Skype, and take them to a virtual lunch or virtual coffee. These sessions shouldn't take more than 30 minutes, and you'll both benefit hugely.

Why? **Because you'll learn firsthand the direct path to their values, interests, and emotional triggers**, and you'll hear it all in their OWN WORDS.

Use THAT language in your marketing because it's much more likely to resonate with other folks just like them!

When you start to sync with your buyers at the deepest and most personal level—and sync up with how they make buying decisions—you're on your way to effective, attractive marketing that will draw clients and customers to you like a magnet.

Note: To download free tools and guides to help you work through the specific ideas in this section, including Understanding Your Prospects Problems, Define Your Value Proposition, and Competitive Positioning Strategy and Action Plan, visit **www.doitmarketing.com/book.**

Leadership and sales expert Stewart Bolno

likes to say that top salespeople always "show up with a bucket, not a microphone." What he means is that you need to **collect** information much more than **give** it.

So listen deeply, take notes carefully, ask more and smarter follow-up questions, and truly absorb both the spoken and unspoken layers of every sales conversation that you have with a real, live prospect.

Because these conversations are increasingly few and far between, you need to maximize the attention and care that you give to every single one! In every situation, you need to listen for people's:

- ✳ Priorities
- ✳ Wants
- ✳ Fears
- ✳ Concerns
- ✳ Requirements
- ✳ Pressures
- ✳ Desires
- ✳ Contingencies
- ✳ Alternatives
- ✳ Relationships
- ✳ Hopes
- ✳ Dreams
- ✳ Aspirations

This goes way beyond the traditional and breezy sales advice to qualify prospects for:

IT'S ABOUT THEM, REALLY

* Need
* Budget
* Authority

Here's an example of a great question: **What are your priorities when looking at products/services like mine?**

Final tip from Stew Bolno: If they answer, "B, 47, and Kangaroos," then DON'T talk about "A, 21, and Buffaloes." Simply ask, **"Which one do you want to talk about first?"**

7 HULA HOOPS® AND KOOL AID®

Imagine for a moment that you have a health condition that is not only serious but that may, in fact, prove to be life threatening.

You jump on the next plane to the internationally known clinic that specializes in curing this and only this rare ailment.

You walk through the lobby and check in with the professional-looking yet friendly staffer behind the desk.

You wait in a well-appointed, modern reception area with phones quietly ringing and a brisk shuffle of patients coming in and out of the examination area. It seems that nobody is kept waiting more than 15 minutes.

Sooner than you expect, your name is called to see the doctor. Your heart is racing, and your palms are sweaty. There's no delicate way to put it: Your life is on the line, and you're putting yourself in the hands of an expert who is about to determine your fate.

After a brief yet thorough examination, and after studying your charts and test results that were sent ahead, the doctor looks up and says, "You can relax. You're going to be absolutely fine. All you have to do is follow two simple treatment steps, and you'll be good as new. And following your treatment, this disease will be gone from your body forever, never to return."

Stop the movie!

Question: **Would you do the two simple steps the doctor is prescribing?** Surgery? Pills? Exercise? Physical therapy? Radiation?

What if the two simple treatment steps went as follows: "For you to be cured of this life-threatening ailment, you need to run out right now into the hospital parking lot and dance with a Hula Hoop®. Then I need you to drink 64 ounces of cherry Kool Aid®."

If you're like most people to whom I pose this question in my Do It! Marketing seminars, you wouldn't hesitate for a moment to dance the hula and drink down that deliciously refreshing beverage.

Why?

Because it's the CURE. It solves your PROBLEM.

At the end of the day, you really don't care WHAT you need to do. You simply want it done so that you get the benefit of the end-result, in this case, avoiding death.

Marketing lesson: Nobody cares about your HOW.

Your assessments, your methodologies, your patented 17-step process, your secret ingredient, your proprietary technology.

That is simply noise. Interestingly, the more you sell your HOW, the more you sound like every other competitor. You lose specialness rather than gain it.

The WHY in this story is simple: to save your life. The HOW doesn't matter a bit. Pills, powders, patented formula, made from Labrador Retriever fur imported from Canada—did you really care? Drink Kool-Aid®, TANG®, or buttermilk—yeah, sure, whatever. **Just pass me the glass!**

REVIEW YOUR MARKETING MATERIALS.

Time to pull out YOUR ads, your website copy, your e-mails. Do you spend those precious few seconds with your prospect talking about YOUR "How" (your methods, inputs, approaches), or do you spend it talking about THEIR "Why" (their needs, outcomes, desires)?

So stop talking about dancing in the parking lot and drinking powdered beverages. In the following space, start talking about saving customers' lives and improving their work in ways that are directly meaningful to THEM:

Before:

_____

_____

After:

_____

_____

8 AVOID BLAH-BLAH-BLAH MARKETING

Sad to say, but most marketing is blah-blah-blah. It goes something like: "We're the best. We have great service. We're dependable. We offer great value. Stop in for great selection, competitive prices, and the personal touch you've come to expect." Blah-blah-blah. That's a whole lotta YOU and nowhere near enough ME.

You know, ME, your customer? The guy with the money? And the problems you might be able to solve? And the friends I could refer you to? Did I mention I'm also the guy who will be in the market soon for your specific product or service? Where's all the stuff about me?

Here's the point: Good marketing is NOT about your business! It's about how your business is different, valuable, and meaningful to customers. It's about _why_ people should do business with you—and **ONLY** you—

because you're the expert in your field. Convey this message effectively and you WON'T have to work with drive-by clients who are a pain to deal with and who run away the second they see a lower price.

DO IT! THREE TESTS TO APPLY TO YOUR MARKETING

1. The Black Marker Test: Put one of your ads (or web pages, brochures, or promo pieces) and one of your competitor's side by side. Now black out both names. Could your piece be mistaken for another company's piece? Could you just cut out the competitor's name and stick your name on it? Might your prospects just not know the difference? If so, you have a piece of blah-blah-blah marketing.

2. The So-What? Test: Take a look at each of your marketing statements in your ads, in your brochures, and on your website. For each point, can you come up with a compelling value-based answer to the question, "So what?"

3. The Prove-It Test: Prospects assume that all marketers are liars. Do you prove any of your claims? How? Do you have testimonials, third-party proof, verifiable facts?

9 STOP SELLING SUGAR

One of my clients is a commercial lender at a community bank. In the middle of a marketing seminar that he attended early in our relationship, we were talking about finding out what his commercial lending customers really want and how to package and position his bank's offerings squarely in the crosshairs of those wants. At one point, he exclaimed with a bit of frustration, "But David—the problem is that I'm selling sugar!"

I turned to the rest of the group and asked, "What's wrong with this picture?"

Everyone agreed that if the *banker* thinks he's selling sugar (a commodity where all that matters is price, price, and price), then the banker is sunk. End of story.

To make your marketing messages click and stick, you have to go back to square one with your marketing strategy and answer some hard questions.

Obviously, if you and your own people believe you're selling sugar, how effective can you be in front of your customers, clients, and prospects in articulating the compelling advantages of doing business with you?

DO IT! QUESTIONS TO HELP YOU STOP SELLING SUGAR

1. Who is your core (best-fit, most desired, highest value) customer?

2. What specific challenges do they face (in their own words)?

3. Who is your competition (including alternatives, comparables, and the status quo)?

4. What are their greatest strengths? What are their weaknesses? (*Hint:* You can't beat them on their weaknesses, only on their strengths!)

5. Who are you (personally, professionally, collectively, and individually)?

6. What do your customers love about you?

7. What do they hate about you?

8. How are you stacking up by the measures your customers care about and in areas your competition may be overlooking?

Spend some time crafting clear, specific answers to these questions—
and then practice them out loud with your team, or with your spouse, or
with your business coach, or with your dog—and you'll soon see a dramatic improvement in the way that your prospects, allies, and referral partners respond to your marketing messages.

10 VISIBILITY + CREDIBILITY = BUYABILITY

Alright, I confess: This section is a little more complicated than the title might suggest. Buyability is when you are using
attractive, effective, relevant, and concise marketing messages, tactics,
and tools. To fully get you and your company's offerings to that state, you
need to see where you currently fall on the Do It! Marketing Nine-Part Buyability Spectrum:

1. Invisible	You're not there when your prospects are looking for your exact type of product, service, or solution. You're not on Google, you're not networking, you're not on the vendor list, you're not at the industry trade show. Total best kept secret (BKS) syndrome. Not good.
2. Visible and annoying	Bad news: This is actually WORSE than being invisible. You're "that guy" desperately handing out business cards at the Chamber. You're the one cold-calling everyone on the association list. You go door to door and put those annoying little cards on my windshield. Everyone hates you. Good news: It's better that you heard it from a friend like me who cares about your success. Stop this idiocy now. Please.

3. Visible and insignificant	You're around. But just barely. Yes, we see your booth at the Chamber Expo. Yes, we get your marketing postcards in the mail. Sure, you show up to the golf outings at the conferences. But you don't *contribute*. You don't make anyone's life or work better because they came into contact with you. You're like a flight attendant standing at the door waving "Buh-bye" like an automaton. You can do better. Keep reading, and you will!
4. Visible and significant	Ah, Level 4—You're moving up! You are not only *visible*, you are now *present* to your customers' and clients' wants, needs, and desires. You show up not only with marketing materials but with solutions, ideas, answers, and insights that your prospects can use—whether they decide to buy from you or not. You're making the world a better place, one significant contribution at a time. You may even be writing articles, blogging, or speaking at your target market's conferences and meetings. Welcome to significance!
5. Visible and credible but not consistent	*Repeatedly* serving your audience with *significance* leads to earning *credibility*. Simply put, customers start to believe in the value that you're sharing with them. You're becoming a trusted source of information, trends, advice, and answers. Problem: You don't do it often enough. A speech every 6 months. The annual article goes out to the magazine. You blog once a month if you're lucky. It's all good, but it's not good *enough* often *enough* to build up to the next phase, which is ...
6. Visible, credible, and consistent	Level 6 comes only from the disciplined use of three calendars: your marketing calendar, your editorial calendar, and your sales calendar. Luckily, we'll dig into these for you later in this book. The point is that you're consistently cranking out top-notch material that solves your target market's urgent, expensive headaches, and heartaches. So they begin to love you for it. So you soon reach...
7. Visible, credible, and buyable	Bingo. Level 7 is where your consistent service to your target market pays off. You're in front of enough prospects with enough value to earn enough attention so that you get the chance to earn more paid work!

8. Visible, credible, and obvious	*Extra Credit 1:* For the overachievers, this level is attained when you provide so much value (online, by phone, in person, with your content, through new customers, with repeat and referral business, via word of mouth, in your enhanced reputation, and consistently great results) that you become the *obvious* choice in your category of product or service. Want a great water bottle? Buy a Camelbak. Need some cool sneakers? Those Nikes are a sure bet.
9. Visible, credible, mistake to buy elsewhere	*Extra Credit 2:* For the serious overachievers, this is the ultimate destination on your visible, credible, buyable scale. The message your prospects and customers receive over and over again is that they *could* buy this product elsewhere, but they'd probably be making a BIG mistake. Think powerful motorcycles: You'd want to get a Harley-Davidson®. Think laser printers, and anything that's not a Hewlitt Packard® would be a mistake. Ketchup? Heinz® without question. Naturally, these are global brands. But there's nothing to stop YOU and your company's products and services from earning the same kind of mistake-to-go-elsewhere status in *your specific target market* with equal marketing impact!

☑ **11** 50 REASONS PEOPLE SHOULD BUY FROM YOU

Time for a stupid question: Do you want to sell
more, sell more easily, and sell more often?

Of course, you do! Every business owner, entrepreneur, and independent professional wants to do that.

Smart question: How do you convey to your PROSPECTS all the different reasons why they should buy from you?

That's the trick. After working through this next exercise, YOU will be able to build yourself one of the most powerful sales tools I've ever seen. (And I've seen a LOT of marketing/sales tools in my 20-plus years in business.)

Because of my involvement in the National Speakers Association (NSA) and the Canadian Association of Professional Speakers (CAPS), I've been fortunate to develop personal friendships with some of the smartest and most successful business speakers, sales experts, and marketing gurus.

One of these folks, Tom Stoyan, is known as Canada's Sales Coach, and he runs the Coaching and Sales Institute (http://CoachingAndSalesInstitute.com). Tom also happens to be a member of the Canadian Speaker's Hall of Fame (HoF). When Tom and I were copresenting at a convention a few years ago, he kindly participated in a small part of my program, and I participated in his. We thought we'd compare notes and both learn a thing or two.

Tom picked up some ideas about social media and inbound marketing, and I learned a million-dollar idea called the Why People Buy from Me Worksheet.

The Worksheet is a structured process that walks you through five key questions, each of which requires 10 answers, giving you an arsenal of 50 selling points. You can use these in your marketing materials, sales conversations, website copy, phone calls, e-mails, and anyplace else you need to

PROVE to your buyers that buying from anyone else would be a HUGE mistake.

As an example, the worksheet for the marketing coaching part of my business follows.

Note: I cheated on Question 3 because I did this exercise from a personal perspective, not from an overall company perspective. If you work for an organization larger than yourself, DO NOT SKIP Question 3. Seek help from your boss and coworkers to answer it, or contact Tom Stoyan and he'll help you answer it as part of his program!

Question 1: Why should I buy your product/service?

1. Because you're terrible at marketing.
2. Because you don't make time for marketing.
3. Because you've read too many books yet implemented too few ideas.
4. Because without proactive marketing, you're the best kept secret at what you do.
5. Because you don't need marketing information; you need marketing implementation.
6. Because you don't know what you don't know about marketing your services.
7. Because you're tired of throwing money in a marketing black hole.
8. Because you want to regain control of your marketing and sales results.
9. Because you're tired of spinning your wheels and you're ready to commit to marketing success.
10. Because you realize that for every marketing dollar you spend, you should get at least $3 in return.

Question 2: Why should I buy from YOU?

1. Because of the powerful testimonials from some of the top entrepreneurs and corporations in the United States.
2. Because I've *been* the services, *bought* the services, and *sold* the services, so I've worked on all three sides of the table!

3. Because I give you the strategies, tactics, and guided implementation you need to generate results.
4. Because my materials, advice, articles, and presentations are splattered all over the web! (You've already heard of me, so I must be doing something right. What if YOU could do the same in your prospect base?)
5. Because I've been quoted or featured in *The New York Times, Investors Business Daily, Fast Company, Selling Power, Sales and Marketing Management, Business 2.0,* and *Entrepreneur* magazine (with a picture!)
6. Because I'm the author of this book, and you're getting dozens of my most powerful business-building ideas. By the time you're done reading them and applying them to your business, you'll know I'm the real deal.
7. Because I've delivered over 600 seminars, presentations, and strategic work sessions since 1992 and I've worked with 44 companies in the Fortune 500.
8. Because I have an application process that you must go through before we work together. I don't work with any warm body with a checkbook.
9. Because my programs are consistently among the highest rated at national conventions and association meetings nationwide.
10. Because I have more than 50 video testimonials on YouTube so you can get firsthand accounts of the impact of my work straight from my clients and audiences.

Question 3: Why should I buy from your company?

1. My company and I are one and the same. See the preceding 10 reasons.

Question 4: Why should I buy at your price?

1. Because I have a 1,000 percent guarantee as follows: "I'm better than anyone who's cheaper; and I'm cheaper than anyone who's better."

2. Pay one price for unlimited coaching and consulting. I'm more concerned about getting you to your destination than running the meter.

3. The fee is the fee. If you're not making back 3–10 times my fee after our work, one of us is not doing his job—and it's not usually me.

4. Everything is too expensive until you want it (Tom Stoyan).

5. People won't spend $50 to fix a $5 problem. But they will spend $1 million to solve a $10 million problem.

6. If you're not comfortable spending big money with me, why would you expect your prospects to spend big money with you?

7. If you ask anyone I've worked with, 90 percent of them will tell you that working with me was some of the smartest money they ever spent. The other 10 percent didn't do the work.

8. You shouldn't work with me if marketing and growing your business is not a serious priority for you.

9. You shouldn't work with me if your business is struggling; get sales coaching first. (I'm serious!)

10. You can spend less, and you'll get less. And you can spend more, and you'll still get less. I overdeliver like crazy (read the testimonials) because once you're "in" with me, I have nothing more to sell you, and we can get to work!

Question 5: **Why should I buy NOW? ("Now is a relative term," Tom Stoyan, 2013).**

1. Because it's rare that I have openings in my client roster. You can get in now or typically wait three to six months.

2. Because the longer you delay getting your marketing house in order, the longer you'll stay in a state of confusion, inaction, and being overwhelmed.

3. Because "waiting till my business picks up" to invest in marketing is like saying, "I'm sick as a dog, but I'll wait till I feel better to go to the doctor." It's never going to happen.

4. I've never seen a marketing plan that starts with "Generate enough sales to afford a marketing plan."

5. Maybe you should never buy, and you might not qualify to work with me.
6. What would it be like if your next year's revenues were much like your last year's? If you're OK with that, there's probably no reason for us to work together.
7. Are you sure you have a marketing problem and not a sales problem? Maybe Stoyan is a better fit for you. Would you like his number?
8. Because the money you're NOT making week after week, month after month, is a larger number than the money you'd be investing to restore your revenues to where you'd like them to be.
9. Because you want to stop the feast-or-famine revenue cycle and get a proactive handle on your marketing process before you hit your next dip.
10. Because someone you know and respect recommended we chat, and I'm the answer to your prayers. (In addition, I'm one of the most humble people you'll ever meet!)

See? I told you it was self-serving.

Until now.

Because NOW it is *your* turn. Here is your assignment:

Why People Buy from Me Worksheet

Question 1: Why should I buy your product/service?
_____
_____

Question 2: Why should I buy from YOU?
_____
_____

Question 3: Why should I buy from your company?
_____
_____

Question 4: Why should I buy your price?

_____

_____

Question 5: Why should I buy *now*?

_____

_____

For a downloadable version of this worksheet, visit **www.doitmarketing.com/book**.

PART THREE

LEARN TO
SPEAK PROSPECT

☑️ **12** BUILD YOUR MARKETING LANGUAGE BANK

Really effective marketing language centers around **speaking "prospect."** That means using the right words that convey to prospects that **you have the answers** to their problems.

Question: Why is marketing language important?

Answer: Think about all the different situations and contexts in which you market your products, services, ideas, and **value** through language. Use the following space to jot down three examples you use regularly in your own business.

Written marketing language:

_____

_____

_____

Spoken marketing language:

_____

_____

_____

Now ask yourself:

Might you be **losing opportunities** by using *product-centered* marketing language versus *prospect-centered* marketing language?

_____

_____

_____

Might you be **losing sales** by not connecting on an emotional level with your buyers?

_____

_____

_____

Do prospects **lower their shields** and WANT to talk with you?

_____

_____

Do you find you're **winging it** when talking with prospects?

_____

_____

_____

Does your language **resonate** with most members of your target market?

_____

_____

_____

Is your marketing language **always** clear, compelling, and consistent?

_____

_____

_____

What the heck is a Marketing Language Bank?

Your _Marketing Language Bank_ is a collection of verbal building blocks that echo your most profitable clients' specific pains, problems, and predicaments before they experienced the improvements provided by your products or services.

How do you use your Marketing Language Bank

The power of your Marketing Language Bank comes from the fact that you invest your time, research, creativity, and effort **once**, and you get to

repurpose, recycle, and reuse your Marketing Language Bank over and over again. *No ad agency required!*

For example, you will dip into your Marketing Language Bank every time you want to...

- Write a **headline** for an ad
- Create a powerful **e-mail** subject line
- Revise your company's **tagline** or **slogan**
- Train your office staff on the kinds of **questions** to ask
- Start a conversation with someone at a **trade show**
- Script your new **telemarketing** campaign
- Develop your **postcard** or **direct mail** strategy
- Write a compelling **blog** post
- Submit an **article** for your industry's trade publication
- Craft a **speech** topic for a national meeting of your target market
- Formalize your customer **referral** program
- Choose **keywords** for your search engine optimization strategy
- Decide on what to write about in your **online press releases**
- Redesign your company's **business cards**
- And on and on and on

Just like investing your money with a real bank where you might have a **checking** account, a **savings** account, and an **investment** account, the different ways you can spend the profits from your Marketing Language Bank are limited only by your imagination.

You will never be facing a blank sheet of paper or a blank computer screen asking yourself, "What do I say about my products or services THIS time?"

It's all been thought-out, pre-developed, and is just **waiting to be deployed**!

In the next few chapters, you will get everything you need to develop your very own Marketing Language Bank that you can use over and over again in all aspects of marketing your business. Let's dig in . . .

✓ **13** SEVEN QUESTIONS TO IDENTIFY YOUR BEST BUYERS

> *"You can spend your precious energy beating down closed doors, or you can choose the doors that open when you knock."*
>
> —Dr. Richard Carlson

A critical part of building your Marketing Language

Bank is to deeply understand your best buyers. This is vital because, after all, the whole purpose of your Marketing Language Bank is to help you **speak prospect language about prospect problems.**

Another way to put this: Market your products, services, ideas, and VALUE to people who are already listening. Use the following space to describe the typical characteristics **of people who are already listening** in your world.

Identifying Your Best Buyers

1. Think about your best clients and customers. WHAT makes them your best?
   _____
   _____

2. What are their job titles? Industries? Affiliations? Traits? Values?
   _____
   _____

3. What problems do they have? What solutions do they SEEK? (State this **in their own words!**)
   _____
   _____

4. Where else have they looked to solve this problem?

_____

_____

5. Why hasn't that worked for them?

_____

_____

6. What do they HATE about your category of product/service or your industry?

_____

_____

7. How can you position yourself as the "Ahh, at last!" solution?

_____

_____

14 DON'T FALL INTO THE SAME-O LAME-O TRAP

As you're drafting your first pass of your Marketing

Language Bank, **you must become keenly self-aware** any time you catch yourself using language that:

- ✳ **Any company could say** and no company can prove. ("We're the best!")
- ✳ **Is overly technical** or jargon filled. ("SaaS 128-bit socket-level redundancy")
- ✳ **Triggers the BS-meter** in your readers. ("Nothing else like it on the planet.")
- ✳ **Makes empty promises.** ("Our difference is our people/quality/service.")
- ✳ **Focuses on a feature,** not a benefit. ("Doors that open a full 130 degrees.")
- ✳ **Focuses on an input,** not an output. ("Our 72-point in-depth recruiting questionnaire.")

* **Sounds like, looks like, or reminds prospects of** a similar product or service from a similar company that does similar work in similar ways. (This is death, and it is all too common. Sorry. There's no nice way to break that news to you!)

Vanilla may be the most popular flavor of ice cream, but vanilla has no place in the way that you articulate the fabulousness of what you and your company do.

Here are two examples (with the names changed to protect both the innocent and the not-so-innocent). See if you can tell which one uses authentic language and which one uses same-o lame-o language.

EXAMPLE 1

XYZ Communications works with nonprofits and foundations to help them reach and educate influential audiences. Our strategies increase the visibility of organizations and the value they provide. We also educate and influence people about why an issue is important and why they should advocate for change.

Our approach is pretty straightforward. While we're focused on strategic communications and problem solving, we're not about long processes or wheel spinning. In the current market, most people want to work quickly to find new and better ways to reach untapped markets or grow existing ones. They want to break through the clutter and have a real impact. That's what we do for the organizations we work with.

We'd like to work with you, too.

EXAMPLE 2

ABC Partners offers proven expertise to help middle-market companies exceed both their short- and long-range goals. Using a flexible model, we provide our clients with the executive talent and tools they need to win in the marketplace, offering them the ability to immediately grow revenue. Simply put, ABC Partners provides an efficient, effective alternative to both develop and successfully execute your competitive strategy.

Which example made you more:

- ✳ Curious?
- ✳ Intrigued?
- ✳ Engaged?
- ✳ Convinced that the firm had a unique offering?
- ✳ Confident they knew what their clients wanted?
- ✳ Likely to pick up the phone or send an e-mail to learn more?

The lesson is fairly simple. The company in Example 2 wrote Same-O Lame-O copy that any of their competitors could clone.

The company in Example 1 kept their language prospect centered, conversational, and approachable. They conveyed that they knew what their best prospects and clients were going through and that they could fix it.

THE COFFEE TEST

It does not take a lot of effort to see whether your marketing language is Same-O Lame-O or not. The first test you might want to try out is the Coffee Test, and it goes like this.

Imagine you are sitting down to have a cup of coffee with a friend, colleague, or referral source. The conversation is casual, comfortable, and friendly. Soon the conversation turns to your business.

The Coffee Test Question: Could you READ your marketing copy from your website or brochure out loud to your prospect without them choking with laughter or staring at you in confusion?

In other words, would you SAY what you've WRITTEN out loud to someone in a face-to-face conversation? If the answer is no, then you need to go back to the drawing board.

The good news is that this test also suggests its own solution to fix all your marketing language in one fell swoop: If you wouldn't say what you've written, then simply **write what you WOULD say!**

Problem solved. You're welcome. And the coffee's on me.

☑ 15 ZERO IN ON YOUR PAIN/GAIN FACTORS

As you continue to work on your Marketing Language Bank, consider applying **three tests** to every market problem you're positioning your product/service to solve. These tests come from authors Craig Stull, Phil Myers, and David Meerman Scott in their brilliant book, *Tuned In*:

1. Is it **urgent**: Are there built-in incentives to solve it now?
2. Is it **pervasive**: Do a lot of people in your target market have it?
3. Is it **expensive:** Does it cost money to have this problem, and are people therefore willing to pay money to solve it?

At this stage, take each of your selling points, features, or benefits, and REVERSE them so each is positioned as **pain relief**, **problem resolution**, and **nightmare prevention.**

Remember to use real **client language** (i.e., in their own words)—**not** marketing speak.

There's no such thing as effective copywriting; it's all about *copy-listening*!

Imagine that you are marketing a new type of sales force automation software system.

You could easily whip up some marketing copy that looks something like this:

With our Prospect Intelligence System, you'll get ...

✳ More consistent leads
✳ Higher conversion ratios
✳ A dashboard of key metrics
✳ Motivation for your superstars
✳ New revenue potential

Warning, warning! Danger, danger! Do you know what this sounds like to most sales managers and VPs? It sounds like blah-blah-blah because EVERY sales force automation ad, website, sales rep, and marketing brochure talks about these same benefits.

Ancient marketing wisdom: If you're going to sell fire extinguishers, first you have to show the fire.

This brings us to one of the most powerful marketing tactics in this book.

Once you learn and develop this next skill, you will become an unstoppable marketing ninja.

It even SOUNDS like a ninja move; it's called **Doing the Flip,** and your mastery of it begins NOW!

Think about this:

> "Feature, features, features ... "
> "Benefits, benefits, benefits ... "

Your prospects have heard this all before. So what can you do to short-circuit their brains to get right past their resistance, cynicism, and defensiveness?

Easy! Talk to them the way they talk to themselves. Read their minds. Echo their own self-talk.

Prove to them that you understand what they're up against: Take your positive features and benefits, and flip them around to become negative conditions they're suffering with (and talking about) right now. Then you'll flip back again with specific pain relief statements that make each of those negatives go away.

Let's walk through the sales force automation example, and you'll quickly see how to do this for your own products and services.

FLIP 1: TAKE YOUR BENEFITS AND **REVERSE THEM**.

What is the **opposite** of each one of your benefits?

More consistent leads	→	Sporadic leads, feast-or-famine sales cycle
Higher conversion ratios	→	Low conversion ratios, missed goals
Dashboard of key metrics	→	No dashboard, data is hard to collect and/or analyze
Motivation for your superstars	→	Demotivated, underperforming superstars
New revenue potential	→	Lost revenue potential, lower profit

FLIP 2: TAKE EACH NEGATIVE AND BUILD A **RESTORATIVE/PAIN RELIEF STATEMENT** AROUND IT.

More consistent leads	Relief from feast-or-famine sales cycles
Higher conversion ratios	Boost low conversion rates back in line with your goals
Dashboard of key metrics	Stop cobbling together sales data scattered in old systems
Motivation for your superstars	Get your best performers unstuck to start winning again
New revenue potential	End the anxiety of slipping revenues and shrinking profits

Doing the Flip

Now it's your turn. Take your favorite piece of your own marketing collateral material. It can be a sales letter, web page, brochure, data sheet, anything.

Go through the Flip process using the space below and convert your current positive benefits to negatives/pains. Then you'll see the underlying problems that your products and services truly solve. Once you have those, powerfully state the restorative pain relief that your product/service provides in plain English.

Positive benefit/outcome:

1. _____
2. _____
3. _____
4. _____

... translates to negative/pain/problem/gap:

1. _____
2. _____
3. _____
4. _____

... gives you specific pain relief/restoration/improvement:

1. _____
2. _____
3. _____
4. _____

Download electronic copies of these tools plus 100 more and a growing library of marketing resources at **www.doitmarketing.com/book**.

16 HOW TO BUILD YOUR PROSPECT PHRASE BOOK

As you're rounding out the final few building blocks of your Marketing Language Bank, you now realize that the whole purpose of this exercise is to STOP talking marketing speak and to START speaking in your new profit-rich dialect known as Prospect.

Once you learn to speak prospect, you'll be much more likely to be seen as a **partner, not a peddler.**

- You'll **gain trust** as you remove hype from your vocabulary.
- You'll **earn respect** as you articulate the exact pains, problems, heartaches, and headaches that your prospects are experiencing, talking about, and seeking help with.
- You'll **get known as a company that gets it** and that can be trusted to deliver solutions through your products, your services, and your value.

Several years ago, I sat down with the CEO of a seven-person IT consulting firm near my home base of Philadelphia. We went out to a local diner for breakfast to chat over bacon and eggs.

We had been introduced by a mutual friend, and neither of us knew whether the connection would lead to business, but we both knew it might if we clicked. After all, he had a need, and I was introduced as a trusted advisor with expertise in marketing and experience in helping professional services firms.

While we're chatting, about halfway through the breakfast, he put down his fork in exasperation and said, "You know, David, I just don't like marketing!" I laughed because that's like my telling him, "You know, Hank, I just don't like techies!" After my chuckle subsided, I asked him to talk more about his dislike for marketing.

The next words that came out of his mouth were pure gold.

He said,: "I don't like marketing because you never know what you're getting. You never know what works. You try some stuff, it flops. You have to put more money in, that doesn't work. Then something you tried six months ago generates a lead, and you just never know what's really going on. I'm tired of throwing money into a marketing black hole."

Pause.

Pick up the fork.

Dig into more bacon.

Luckily, I was listening. REALLY listening.

Go back to Idea 13. Hank had just done a brilliant job of answering Questions 6 and 7 of my buyer persona questions. "What do they HATE about your category of product/service or your industry?" "How can you position yourself as the "Ahh, at last!" solution?"

After we finished breakfast and said our good-byes, I went back out to my car.

I got in, closed the door, and grabbed the pen and pad that are always in my glove box. I wrote down VERBATIM what Hank said. There were four or five real gems, but I circled his one phrase, "I'm tired of throwing money into a marketing black hole."

Fast-forward to today. Featured prominently on my marketing services page is the result of developing my own Marketing Language Bank **after hearing the same complaint from dozens of executives and entrepreneurs** just like Hank:

"PROFESSIONAL SERVICES MARKETING? NO THANKS! I'M TIRED OF THROWING MONEY INTO A MARKETING BLACK HOLE."

As a professional services firm principal, managing partner, CEO, president, or practice leader, is this you?

- ✳ **"We always get beat up on price because we have no credibility with prospects who've never heard of us before."**

- ✳ **"I'm constantly asked for new marketing tools, brochures, and presentations, but nothing seems to help."**

> ❋ "How do I know which marketing strategies and tools will help us close more sales?"
>
> ❋ "There has to be a more systematic way we can market our products/services."
>
> ❋ "There are so many new ways to reach buyers these days; should we be using social media, blogs, podcasts, video? And do any of those even work in our industry?"

A few months later, Hank was considering hiring a marketing firm. He visited our website once more, and when I sat down to meet with him a few days later, he said, "Obviously you know what we're going through. I was looking around on your website, and it felt like you were talking specifically to ME." He hired us. We did some great work together. Money in the bank.

Three words of advice for you: Authentic. Client. Language.

DO IT!: HOW TO GATHER AUTHENTIC CLIENT LANGUAGE

Live in *their* world, think about *their* problems, and think about *their clients and prospects.*

What's the first step? Research. Preparation. Homework.

Industry, regional, business, and company news is now at everyone's fingertips on the Internet. Look for verbatim quotes, video clips, and audio interviews to capture as much as you can. Then go directly to the source— **your real live customers and prospects.**

After all, if you're not **intelligently researching your prospects' issues, challenges, and pressures**, how can you possibly come up with credible high-perceived-value solutions?

One of the best ways to approach prospects is with:

- Interviews
- Surveys
- Research
- Data gathering

This positions your company as an expert resource and gives you valuable data you should be getting anyway.

Finally, of course, you have the **informal, in-person tools of breakfast, lunch, dinner, and coffee with your current and prospective clients.** Just be sure to bring a digital audio recorder, or be prepared to take good notes. Once they start talking prospect language about prospect problems, your mind will be reeling with all the possible ways you can deploy their sound bites in your Marketing Language Bank!

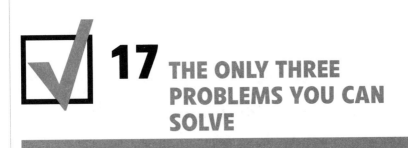

17 THE ONLY THREE PROBLEMS YOU CAN SOLVE

You may sell the world's greatest widgets. You may have patented the most efficient doodad your industry has ever seen.

Your flagship service may be the most effective on the planet with the only 100 percent bulletproof guarantee in the business.

Hard truths:

- None of your prospects has a widget problem.
- None of your prospects has a doodad deficiency.
- None of your prospects stay up at night searching for a bulletproof guaranteed service.

You and your company can solve only three problems. And solving those three problems specifically, quickly, and profitably is your MAIN and ONLY job, assuming you want to make the **greatest contribution** to your clients and truly serve them in a way that translates to **their bottom line** so that they want to pay you **enormous amounts of money.**

Would you like to know what these three problems are?

Sure you would. So the next three chapters lay out your new mission, mantra, and focus...

For every... Single... Thing... Your Company... Sells...

Let's say you're about to sit down with a corporate decision maker.

This is a top executive, maybe the CEO, maybe a senior VP, but definitely someone with an executive position AND check-writing authority for what you market and sell.

Depending on the size of the company, you might want to start with one or more questions like these:

* ✸ **"You have a whole portfolio of products and services and programs. What are the two or three top drivers as you see them?"** (*Note:* CEOs love this kind of talk!)

* ✸ **"And what are the two or three initiatives that you're putting a lot of resources behind and that absolutely have to be successful for you to look back on this year as a banner year?"**

* ✸ **"Imagine you have a whole dashboard. Which two or three needles are you looking to move?"**

The prospect lays out the situation, and you ask a few follow-up questions to flesh out the answers. Then ask a question like this one: "Based on everything that you can see from where you're sitting [a nice nod to their power that suggests they're sitting on their throne!], what are two or three of the biggest obstacles in your way?"

They may answer right away, or they might ask you for clarification. At that point, you bring out the big guns and say, "Well, typically we're brought in when people in your position are up against one or more of these three problems: **people problems, process problems, and profit problems.** Which is the most relevant one for you?"

Some good follow-up questions are:

* Where are your competitors nipping at your heels?
* In what areas are you winning today and want to move even further ahead?
* What are some internal challenges?
* How do your good ideas sometimes get derailed?
* What are the black holes in your organization [i.e., where ideas and projects go to die]?
* What are some process problems?
* Where would you like to grease the wheels and get things rolling more smoothly?

Once you have the basics of the situation in hand, you can then begin to work in the Three P's sales conversation centering around **People, Process and Profit**.

Let's dig into people problems first.

☑ **18** YOU SOLVE PEOPLE PROBLEMS

As you're leading the sales conversation with your

prospect, you can talk specifically about people obstacles (not individual people but their *people issues* that are acting as obstacles). You want to get the lay of the land to understand what they're up against.

People problems come in all shapes and sizes, but here's a starter list so that you can talk more intelligently about them with your prospects:

* Recruiting top talent
* Retaining top talent
* Employee engagement

- 🟆 Recognition and reward
- 🟆 Staff utilization
- 🟆 Leadership
- 🟆 Teamwork
- 🟆 Communication
- 🟆 Coaching
- 🟆 Collaboration
- 🟆 Succession
- 🟆 Silos and turf wars
- 🟆 Gossip, gab, and the grapevine
- 🟆 Delegation
- 🟆 Micromanagement
- 🟆 Perfectionism
- 🟆 Negativity
- 🟆 Entitlement
- 🟆 Arrogance
- 🟆 Complacency

No matter what you sell—commercial, industrial, retail, wholesale, manufacturing, distribution, products, services, programs, ideas—they can ALL be tied to one or more of these underlying people problems, risks, or gaps.

Yes, really.

In fact, if you're not talking about these, you're positioning your product or service or solution as a nice-to-have and NOT as a must-have.

Decision makers ALWAYS need to solve SOME of these problems and make improvements in the rest of them. They do NOT always need your product or service.

Tie them TOGETHER—and you win.

✓ 19 YOU SOLVE PROCESS PROBLEMS

Process problems **show up as inefficiencies, gaps,** missed opportunities, too much wasted time or effort, too many steps, too much bureaucracy or paperwork, or too many layers between customer and company.

Entire industries have been built around business process innovation. And a handful of fads from the 1950s to the 1990s didn't help: the total quality movement, business process reengineering, outsourcing, insourcing, rightsizing. You name it.

Let's cut to the chase and catalog a brief list of potential sources of process problems that you may want to discuss with your prospect in order to get their attention focused on the desired OUTPUT of investing in your company's products or services:

- Accounting
- Billing
- Call Centers
- Contracting
- Customer Service
- Delivery
- Distribution
- Engineering
- Facility Management
- Finance
- Information Systems
- Innovation
- Inventory Management
- Manufacturing
- Marketing
- Operations
- Payroll

- Product Development
- Regulatory Compliance
- Research and Development
- Sales
- Strategic Planning
- Workforce Diversity

Tie some of these into your sales conversations and again, you win!

20 YOU SOLVE PROFIT PROBLEMS

Profit problems come in many shapes and sizes.

What's important is that, when you are marketing and selling your products and services, you do NOT overlook this vitally important problem. It is NEVER far from the mind of any serious decision maker. If profitability is NOT a big deal to your prospect, then you are talking to the wrong prospect!

Often placed at the end of a chain reaction of internal and external variables (where your products and services come into play) when you talk about solving your customers' profitability problems, the outcomes almost always end up with YOU using the following "so-that" phrases:

- So that you sell more
- So that you sell more often
- So that you sell at full price
- So that you avoid discounting
- So that you open new markets
- So that you expand your product line

- So that you cut costs
- So that you manufacture and distribute more efficiently
- So that you speed up time to market
- So that you cross-sell
- So that you up-sell
- So that you open new channels
- So that you raise prices
- So that you boost your margins
- So that your per-unit cost goes down
- So that you franchise
- So that you license
- So that your stock price goes up
- So that you conserve more cash

SPOILER ALERT

If your business solves **people** problems, you may have been saddened to see all the **process** and **profit** problems just now. Here's a secret: 100 percent of these problems are PEOPLE problems in disguise.

Why? Because **someone owns** the screwed-up process and hasn't fixed it. **Someone else owns** the unprofitable business unit, product, or service—and cannot or will not face the problem, deal with the consequences, and fix it. So if you solve people problems, you can have marketing conversations on ALL of these levels, and you get three chances to make your case!

21 CONTROL IS PRICELESS

When you're marketing to high-powered executives, professionals, or entrepreneurs, you can rarely go wrong by highlighting how your product or service enhances their level of control in their business.

Think about it: Control is at the core of what every Alpha Dog executive and entrepreneur wants.

Not only control over their business, but also control over their finances, control over their people, control over their processes, control over their customers, and control over their suppliers. These people want to control the world.

And you should figure out ways to help them do exactly that.

After all, control is a buffer against fear. Control is a shield against uncertainty. And control is a powerful antidote to doubt.

Position your offerings not in terms of saved money or earned money, not in terms of less wasted time or more free time, but simply in terms of MORE control and LESS chaos. Do that, and you will have sold the ultimate benefit to most of your prospects: the protection they seek from fear, uncertainty, and doubt.

Don't underestimate the power of this angle in every marketing message, every sales conversation, and every carefully chosen question you ask during your sales process. Use this one lever, and you'll soon see the floodgates open and your closing ratio skyrocket because you're speaking the language of control.

Give me more time—great. Give me more money—exciting. Give me more control—priceless.

☑ **22** YOUR BUYERS ARE LAZY, BUSY, AND BEFUDDLED

Marketing and selling have become even more challenging because—now more than ever—your buyers are lazy, busy, and befuddled.

See if some of these characteristics ring true with YOUR prospects and buyers:

LAZY

Your buyers do not look forward to being marketed and sold to. The old standards of *good, cheap,* and *fast* have been replaced with the new so-called web 2.0 standard of *perfect, free,* and *now. Instant gratification, easy to buy*, and *effortless to install* are the new watchwords for marketing and sales success. **The expert at hand is the expert who gets hired.**

BUSY

Buyers have a million things on their plate besides researching the best options for products, services, vendors, partners, and trusted advisors. You need to become the **obvious choice, the smartest choice, and the least risky choice**—all in the span of a very short amount of time to be heard above their (internal and external) noise.

BEFUDDLED

Buyers are overwhelmed with information, choices, data, specs, features, benefits, and marketing hype. Your buyers have been burned, disappointed, and let down by slick marketers in the past. Their shields are up. You won't win them over with sizzle. So, you must convey TWO things with the utmost clarity and conviction:

1. **You understand what they're up against**
2. **You can fix it**

DO IT! THREE WAYS YOUR BUSINESS CAN MARKET TO THE LAZY, BUSY, AND BEFUDDLED

Market to the lazy: What can you OFFER that's easy, fast, and free?

Example on your attorney website: "Click here to download our free guide, *17 Mistakes in Hiring a Lawyer and How to Avoid Them.*"

Market to the busy: What can you DO to be heard above the noise?

Example for your IT firm: "We are the ONLY firm that offers a *100 percent money-back guarantee* that your project will be completed in 90 days. If it's not, you don't pay."

Market to the befuddled: What can you SAY that will immediately resonate with your best prospects because it shows that you "get" them?

Example in your consulting sales letters: "We know you've been burned and disappointed by consultants before. So have we. Over half our clients come to us specifically because another firm botched their project, took way too long, went way over budget—*or all three.*"

23 CLARITY INDICATES EXPERTISE

Clarity indicates expertise.

The more clear and concise you can be, the more you'll gain the halo effect of expertise, quality, reliability, effectiveness, and value.

How concise can you make your pitch?

How soon can you stop talking and start listening?

Cut the fat and try to say 50 percent LESS.

Less is more.

Less sells more.

Truly.

DO IT! SUCCESS STRATEGY: WHAT A NINE-YEAR-OLD CAN TEACH YOU ABOUT SALES CLARITY

Tom Searcy

A recent study confirmed my suspicion that most people don't remember what we present to them in a sales call. The data suggested that the average buyer in a meeting will remember only one thing—one!—a week after your meeting.

Oh, and by the way: You don't get to choose what that one thing is. Sigh.

So what have business owners, entrepreneurs, and sales professionals done about this? They have worked on "honing the message," developing a "compelling unique advantage," and, of course, the ultimate silver bullet: "a surefire elevator pitch."

But here's what you're fighting: a world cluttered with information, schedules packed with more meetings and work than a person can handle, and a decision-making process with more people involved in every choice, many of whom know little about your product or service. No wonder so little is remembered; often your audience doesn't even understand much about what you're offering.

What kids want to know

My nine-year-old daughter has spring freckles, long brown hair, and blue eyes the size of silver dollars. She asks the kinds of questions that on the surface seem so simple:

- Daddy, what do you do?
- Why do people decide to hire you?
- Why don't they hire somebody else or do it themselves?

One of the great things about nine-year-olds is that, like many prospects these days, they lack context. Any answer that you provide has to be in a language that they can understand.

What does a procurement specialist know about what you sell—or the IT person, or the finance person? The challenge is this: Can you answer the three questions my nine-year-old asked, for your own business?

Hint: There are right and wrong answers for all of them.

Daddy, what do you do?

Right answer: "I help companies to grow really fast by teaching them how to sell bigger companies much larger orders."

Wrong answer: "Our company helps develop inside of our clients a replicable and scalable process for them to land large accounts."

Why do people decide to hire you?

Right answer: "We have helped lots of companies do this before, so we are really good at it, as long as they are the right type of companies."

Wrong answer: "We have a proven process for implementation that allows organizations to tailor the model to their market, business offering, and company's growth goals."

Why don't they do it themselves?

Right answer: "Just like when you learned to play the piano: Mommy and I could teach a little, but we don't know as much as your teacher, and teaching you ourselves would take a long time and be very frustrating. Daddy's a really good teacher of how to make bigger sales, and people want to learn how to do this as fast as they can."

Wrong answer: "We are the foremost expert in this field with over $5 billion in business that our clients have closed using this system. Usually our clients have tried a number of things on their own before we work together and have wanted outside help to get better results."

In these cases, both answers are accurate, but that doesn't make them *right*.

In a world in which more decisions are made with less information and context, your responsibility is to get to as clear and memorable an answer as possible for all of your buyers to understand.

Tom Searcy, coauthor of the McGraw-Hill book, *How to Close Deals Like Warren Buffett*, is an expert on key account sales strategy. With his sales strategy company, Hunt Big Sales, Tom has helped clients land more than $5 billion in deals. Tom is the author of *RFPs Suck! How to Master the RFP System Once and for All to Win Big Business* and the coauthor of *Whale Hunting: How to Land Big Sales and Transform Your Company*. Connect with Tom at www.HuntBigSales.com.

PART FOUR

EXPERT POSITIONING

24 HOW TO PROFIT FROM 3PR

If you want to win new business from new clients, speaking is one of the most effective tools in your toolkit for burnishing your expert credentials.

By the time you're done reading this chapter, you will understand how to unleash the power of 3PR in your business development efforts, including the number one strategy: speaking.

3PR (Personalized Professional Public Relations) is a combination of strategies, tactics, and tools designed to help you and your business accomplish one or more of these seven key business objectives:

1. New lead generation
2. Building credibility and brand preference
3. Connecting with media and industry analysts
4. Opportunities to engage your top talent
5. Management development
6. Thought-leading content creation
7. Contribution to your professional community

Let's unpack specifically what we mean by **3PR—Personalized Professional Public Relations:**

* **Personalized:** Your firm is made up of individuals. Each member of your team has specific strengths, capabilities, preferences, and a personality that can be leveraged in marketing, positioning, and amplifying the messages that your firm wants to impress on the prospects, clients, and influencers in your target markets.

* **Professional:** 3PR has one goal: professional exposure for your firm's expertise, products, services, and value proposition. Many business leaders shy away from the spotlight of 3PR, asserting, "It's not about me." Although

this is true, it certainly IS about YOU providing value, expertise, and guidance to help your target market succeed.

* **Public:** Your team may be top-notch with proven expertise that generates amazing results for your clients. However, if you don't make your expertise public, you will suffer what many executives and entrepreneurs describe in frustration as "Best Kept Secret Syndrome." 3PR puts your expertise in front of prospects—exactly where it belongs if you want to generate new business more easily and more often.

* **Relations:** Stop thinking in terms of closing the sale, and focus rather on building relationships with your audiences, readers, followers, and fans. The content that you share in a typical 3PR campaign is useful, valuable, actionable, specific, and insightful. Do this consistently, and you'll build trust, likeability, and a reputation for excellence. So when a need arises, you and your firm will be on speed dial, and your prospects will consider it a serious mistake to hire anyone else.

Here are the three pillars of a typical 3PR campaign:

* **Speaking:** Target profit-rich speaking engagements in front of audiences composed of high-probability prospects. Then develop a "marketing magnet" presentation that will engage, attract, and convert prospects to take the next step in your new client acquisition process.

* **Writing:** Write articles, white papers, special reports, blogs, tip sheets— anything that your prospects will find valuable and relevant. You and your firm need to become known for creating and sharing a consistent stream of high-quality information that solves your prospect's problems. Yes, even before they hire you! (*Note:* Traditional PR—placing articles in hardcopy and digital venues that your prospects read and respect—although possibly important for your firm is generally icing on the cake since the web has turned ALL of us into publishers.)

* **Social media:** Social media platforms such as Twitter, LinkedIn, Google+, and YouTube now generate up to 40 percent of the website traffic for successful entrepreneurial companies. If you and your firm are not taking advantage of these social media platforms to offer value and invite engagement with your target market, you are missing a significant opportunity to generate new leads and stimulate meaningful prospect conversations.

The overall impact of a 3PR campaign can be boiled down to one word: expertizing.

Expertizing is the cumulative effect of your speaking, writing, and social media efforts. Taken to the extreme, it might even result in your writing a nonfiction business book to position you and your firm as thought leaders.

Expertizing includes the ability of SEVERAL of your firm's leaders to clearly and confidently deliver a kick-ass presentation at trade shows, conferences, and industry events.

And it includes positioning you and your company's key leaders as experts via your website, videos, media kits, social media presence, articles in trade publications, regular blogging. You might even establish an internal speaker's bureau function to more efficiently pursue, track, and land speaking engagements for your key executives in front of audi-ences that matter.

How successful are you at using these 3PR strategies to drive your business credibility, visibility, and revenue?

And do you do it once in a while with mixed results or in between proj-ects when you have spare time to fill?

If your company is already consistently doing a great job, welcome to the 1 percent club. If not, consider creating a simple 3PR plan to put these pieces in place for your company's future marketing success.

☑ **25** CEO SPEAKING IS YOUR BEST WEAPON

THE CHALLENGE

Too often, small business owners and professional services firms:

* Do marketing by accident or don't do outbound marketing effectively
* Hope that "prospects will call us when they need us"
* Never know where their next lead is coming from
* Don't market using their best asset— thought leadership
* Throw too many dollars into a marketing black hole

THE OPPORTUNITY

Independent research with over 700 services firms proves that the number one source of new business is "making warm calls to existing clients" and that the number two and three sources are "speaking at conferences and trade shows" and "running our own seminars and events." Yet if your business is like most, you haven't yet cracked the code on how to make this work for *your* people to attract *your* clients.

According to the Wellesley Hills Group, *What's Working in Lead Generation* professional services market study, **52–72 percent of B2B professional services BUYERS are willing to switch to new service providers** across a spectrum of specialties.

Meaning: You're always ONE good presentation away from closing new business.

So how can you make that happen for you and your company?

The most successful executives and entrepreneurs become recognized thought leaders in their areas of expertise because they deploy three powerful tools every time they speak: Clarity, Expertise, and Openness. These are the keys to CEO speaking:

✸ **Clarity:** In any speaking situation, clarity indicates *power*, *confidence*, and *capability*. Less is more. Convey a few points powerfully. Focus your message, and, like a laser beam, it will cut through even the most steely prospects you're likely to encounter.

✸ **Expertise:** Expertise has replaced dollars as your marketing investment. *Those who share the most value win*. Actionable, specific, do-this-now strategies and tactics are the coin of the realm. This goes beyond educating your prospects and even goes so far as setting the buying criteria or helping them do it themselves if they so choose.

✸ **Openness:** Openness is about collaboration. Marketing is no longer someone yelling through a megaphone. It's a person-to-person conversation. Forget about being the source of all information to your clients. Your new job is to open the possibilities, ask great questions, and then serve as a filter, lens, and curator. Openness means that every time you speak, you speak *with* them; you don't do it *to* them!

26 FIND OUT WHICH AUDIENCES PAY OFF

Question: Which groups do your ideal clients belong to? The answer will obviously determine which audiences you want to be in front of.

Don't guess—**ask!**

Here is the script to ask your current clients, prospects, and centers of influence who know your target market well.

> **"I'm looking to speak more in front of groups of [buyer persona]. I'd love to get your advice, insights, and recommendations."***

Here's another way to ask.

> **"Of all the industry groups and associations you belong to, which ones provide the most value in terms of the speakers and programs they present?"**

With both scripts, the natural follow-up discussion would center on your desire to serve this industry or community more and to share information with them that would help them become even more successful.

Likely outcomes from this discussion:

* Names of specific groups, associations, and conferences
* Names of specific people serving in board or programming positions
* Names of other executives or decision makers in the field

---

*Asking for "advice, insights, and recommendations" is a technique from my speaking colleague, Michael Goldberg, CSP. Hire him. He's awesome.

- Names of other organizations in need of similar expertise
- Specific networking introductions
- Offers of referrals to the individuals they already know
- An opportunity to reciprocate and ask how YOU might be of service to THEM

The good news: Any or all of these will put you miles ahead of where you would have been if you had not asked at all!

The bad news: Finding venues to speak at profitably can be like trying to find a needle in a haystack. For a free list of resources to help you laser-target your speaking to your best-fit audiences, visit **http://www.doit-marketing.com/book.**

DO IT! SUCCESS STRATEGY: 10 WAYS TO WIN CLIENTS

Henry DeVries, MBA

Do you want to build a reputation to woo and win clients? Some of the quickest reputation-building routes involve talking and typing. You should host workshops, give speeches, and get published.

Competency will not win you clients. Clients today are bombarded with articles, lectures, and seminars that contain generalities and do not distinguish the author or presenter from the competent competition. The secret is to demonstrate that you have something to offer that your competitors do not.

The answer is a neglected learning tool: conducting proprietary research on topics of interest to prospective clients. You don't have to be a marketing research expert to pull this off.

Here is a 10-step action plan to put this learning-into-earning strategy to work for you:

1. Conduct proprietary research you can use in seminars and publicity. Remember those lectures in science class about the scientific method?

Well, it's time to dust off that knowledge. The scientific method is about observing, forming a theory (or hypothesis), and then experimenting to test the results.

2. From your experience and observations, pick the three biggest problems you solve for clients, and turn each problem into a research topic.

3. Ask yourself: "Will this research be relevant to potential clients and trade journal editors?" If no, rethink the topic. If yes, proceed.

4. Surf the web to review the literature of books, articles, and published studies that relate to your research topic. Collect data through opinion surveys, focus groups, and analysis of case studies. Probably the best thing you can do is interview about a dozen people who match the description of your target client. Tell them you are using the information to write an article (you are).

5. Analyze the data to draw conclusions and make recommendations. Write a summary report on the findings of your research. (This can be as simple as a report or as elaborate as a book.)

6. Use the research information in your seminars, speeches, how-to articles, website content, and publicity.

7. From the research and your experience, create your own defined problem-solving system that will help you attract clients. Outline what you already do to solve client problems. Then break this process down into a series of defined steps (usually from five to seven are enough).

8. Give the process an intriguing name, typically no more than four words. Begin with "The" and end with "System," "Process," or "Methodology" for your proprietary process name.

9. Search Google and the U.S. Patent Office website (www.uspto.gov) to find out whether you can trademark the name (steer clear if it's already been used in your industry). Seek legal protection of the process as intellectual property through the U.S. Patent Office. You can hire an attorney to help you or do it yourself based on the instructions on the Patent Office website.

10. Include the process on your website, but give only enough detail to describe it in general, so that you have room to adapt it for each selling situation. Also include the process in your speeches, seminars, and proposals. Continually improve the process, and be sure to document the improvements.

Why should potential clients listen to you? Because you have the research on how they compare to their peers. That is how you can convert the curious into clients. Like the old pastor once said, you can't save souls in an empty church.

Henry DeVries, founder of the New Client Marketing Institute, is the coauthor of the McGraw-Hill book *How to Close Deals Like Warren Buffett*. The former agency president of an Ad Age 500 firm, DeVries is on the marketing faculty and is the assistant dean of continuing education at the University of California San Diego. He is a newspaper columnist and the coauthor of *Self-Marketing Secrets, Pain Killer Marketing,* and *Closing America's Job Gap*. He earned his MBA at San Diego State University and completed certificate programs at the Harvard Business School.
Connect with Henry at www.NewClientMarketing.com.

27 BE SERIOUS

My guess is that you're not taking yourself seriously enough. As a business owner. As a thought leader. As a trusted advisor.

Let's do a quick check to find out for sure.

Five Clues that you're not serious (enough)

1. Your e-mail address ends in @aol.com.
2. You don't have a personal website or blog for you or your work, ideas, and services.
3. Your business cards have those little perforated edges.
4. You say you're a business owner, but you also sell real estate on the side and have a thriving e-Bay business selling collectible figurines. And you sell used boats on weekends.
5. You say that you love what you do, you just don't like the marketing part.

DO IT! BECOME A MORE SERIOUS, MORE CREDIBLE EXPERT

If you agree (and even if you don't), please list five more ways you are going to start becoming more serious, more credible, and more presentable as an expert in your field.

1. _____
2. _____
3. _____
4. _____
5. _____

Forget about working harder.
Success often comes from just *thinking harder!*

Before others will take you seriously as an expert, you first have to take yourself seriously. So pay attention to your **expert image and presentation!**

DO IT! SUCCESS STRATEGY: BOOST YOUR BUSINESS WITH PRESS RELEASES

Dan Janal

Press releases can be a great tactic to get more visitors to your website, where you can build trust and make more sales. Not only are press releases printed in newspapers and magazines, but now they are indexed on search engines so that your customers and prospects can see them online as well.

Many business owners and entrepreneurs mistakenly think a press release can only contain news, such as announcing a new product, hiring a new executive, or winning an award.

True, those were the bread and butter of press releases in the past, but today your press releases can contain many more interesting topics that can help you get free publicity.

Here are five topics for press releases that you should consider writing.

1. Press releases don't have to be based on news. They just need to be interesting. That's why you see successful companies use feature articles and information articles as press releases. That's because newspapers and magazines WANT feature articles and how-to articles. These press releases help reporters who write those kinds of stories.

2. Press releases can be based on opinion. If you want to take issue with a government policy, a research report, or a new book's thesis, you can do so in a press release. These press releases help position you as a thought leader who is unafraid to buck conventional thinking.

3. Press releases can be short. If you can tell your story in 100 words, then do so. A simple job promotion or an event can be told by answering the six who, what, when, where, why, and how questions that should be the cornerstone of any press release.

4. Press releases can be long. In the old days, newspapers had a limited size. On the Internet, space is not an issue. You can tell your story in as much detail as you like. Of course, people have limited attention spans, so you might want to take that into account. On the other hand, people who have a vested interest in your issue or topic will want to read as much info as they can get their hands on.

5. You can write a press release yourself. Just find a good one you like on the Internet, and use that as a template. Or you can hire a PR person to write the press release for you. Make sure the person has a good background in business news and writing so that your press release looks and sounds professional. If reporters think the press release is amateurish, they'll throw it away.

Press releases can be a great way to attract new prospects and make more sales.

If you follow these tips, you'll have lots of great ideas to write press releases to promote your small business.

Dan Janal, author of *Reporters Are Looking for You!*, helps small businesses get publicity so that they can sell more products and services. His clients get terrific results from his coaching, consulting, done-for-you services, and do-it-yourself tools. For information, go to www.prleadsplus.com or call Dan at 952-380-1554.

28 CHASING CHUM MAKES YOU A CHUMP

It's amazing how many business owners, entrepreneurs, and independent professionals fall right into the marketing trap of overt self-promotion, pathetic begging, and self-commoditization.

What am I talking about?

I belong to several online forums, special interest sites, and private message boards for organizations like the National Speakers Association, Sales and Marketing Executives International, and Vistage, the world's largest CEO organization.

At least weekly, requests surface for referrals to various types of consultants, vendors, and professional services firms.

And, as surely as the sun rises in the East and sets in the West, there are desperate goofballs who emerge from the murkiness and respond like hungry sharks chasing chum in bloody waters.

Instead of positioning themselves as experts and giving the referrals as asked, they see these requests as opportunities to play their favorite game of "Pick me! Pick me!"

Here is a recent example from a private Group Discussion on LinkedIn:

> **I'm working with a client who needs a keynoter on growth (franchise-related, if possible). Can anyone recommend a fantastic and engaging executive-level speaker on this topic?**

❋ Response 1: I am a professional speaker with topics from communication, diversity and personal and business growth. My firm has grown 15 percent in the last year, so I have some insights into the topic.

❋ Response 2: We work extensively with franchise organizations on business growth, strategy, and marketing. I'd be happy to explore whether the vast body of knowledge we have about franchise growth in our industry might be adapted to your client.

❋ Response 3: I'm a former VP with Hilton Worldwide. Specifically for the Homewood Suites by Hilton brand. I played an integral role in helping double the Brand's size—from 75 properties to 150—in a four-year period. Not sure if the hospitality industry would be an optimal choice for your client, nonetheless I'd be happy to hear more about your client's needs.

❋ Response 4: There is a fantastic niche bureau in the franchise world run by Katrina Mitchell—these folks are extremely well-versed in the franchise world: http://www.franchisespeakers.com. Also, T. Scott Gross would be a home run for this type of group as well—which is why he's among the folks Katrina works with!

❋ Response 5: I'm both a speaker and a retail franchise owner, so I may be a good fit if they are still looking. I'm a leadership keynoter who focuses on building trust in teams. I also own two franchises and am in the process of expanding into a third. View my profile for more info if I can help.

I'll stop there only because quoting more of these people would make me nauseated.

Lesson: There was only ONE "trusted advisor" answer in the whole bunch. Can you see which one it was? It was the one that gave the requester what she WANTED—namely, a REFERRAL and not a self-serving sales pitch.

The definition of a trusted advisor is a professional who puts her client's interests before her own.

Responders 1, 2, 3, and 5 position themselves as PEDDLERS, not PARTNERS.

Remember: Chasing chum makes you a chump.

Don't do it.

You have three smarter approaches.

1. **Ask one of your clients for whom you have done similar work** to visit that forum and post an honest recommendation of your work. A third-party endorsement means a TON more than a self-serving sales pitch.
2. **Take the conversation offline.** Connect the referral requester with the person you'd like to refer. (Or if you're back to promoting yourself, then simply connect your past client with the requester's contact details and ask the client to get in touch directly.)
3. **Trade referrals and endorsements.** This is one of my favorites. It is **smarter** than self-promotion and **easier** than reconnecting with previous clients. Establish a trusted circle of five to seven other business owners, executives, or professional services providers whose work you believe in and who would gladly get behind your reputation. Offer to tee each other up regularly for opportunities like the one above.

In my circle, for example, I have:

* A women's leadership guru whose message focuses on women's sanity, confidence, and fun.
* A *New York Times* best-selling health-care author and Hall of Fame speaker.
* One of the nation's top experts on building sales culture.
* A top-notch trainer on presentation skills (virtual and in person).
* One of the funniest motivational humorists on the planet.
* A networking and referral expert focused on the insurance and real estate industries.
* A small business leadership expert, best-selling author, and Hurricane Katrina survivor.

Stop chasing chum and you'll stop looking like a chump.

Question: Who is in YOUR referral circle? Get busy and create yours today!

PART FIVE

DOMINATE
SOCIAL MEDIA

29 CREATE KILLER SOCIAL MEDIA SCRIPTS

The LAST thing I ever want to be called is a social media expert." Yech. That ain't what I do, and it ain't who I am. Ain't. Ain't. Ain't.

There, that feels better. Now what I AM is a social media enthusiast. I love it, and I think it's a great tool to add to your Internet marketing game plan.

Is it **perfect** for everyone? No.

Is it **useful** for some? Yes.

Is it **vital** for a few? Certainly.

So, to help you ramp up the effectiveness of your social media efforts, **you need to know what to say and how to say it.**

Most of the initial contact templates that these social media tools offer—like the standard LinkedIn connection invite, the Facebook friend connection, and others—are pretty weak.

No worries, you're about to get hooked up with some killer social media scripts you can adapt for yourself to become much MUCH more effective at building your online tribe.

LINKEDIN

Quick Marketing 101 review: Do people care about YOU, or do they care about themselves? Yes—that's right! Five points. They don't give a rat's ass about you, and they care 100 percent about themselves.

Now look at the standard LinkedIn connection invite:

> *I'd like to add you to my professional network on LinkedIn.*

Hmmmm. How do you feel about being "added"? And who cares about "my professional network"? This is all wrong.

Here's your new template. Notice the **switch in focus and benefit.** Plus I added a new line with even *more value*:

> *I'd like to put my professional network on LinkedIn at your disposal. After we connect, if there's someone to whom you'd like a personal introduction, just let me know. Thanks in advance.*

FACEBOOK

You can't really go wrong here, but I still have a useful connection script for you.

Notice that, on your Facebook friends list, people connected to your friends are listed with labels like "37 mutual friends," "51 mutual friends," and so on.

You can connect with these folks, but the chances are excellent that they might not know you from Adam or Eve. Thus, you need a fun, approachable, and appealing script when you want to click on them to connect. After you click on "Add as Friend," click on the link in the dialog box that says, "Add a personal message." Then type:

> *Vanessa—Wow! We have 85 mutual friends. We GOTTA connect simply so we can talk about all these people!*

TWITTER

First rule: **Don't use automatic direct messaging (DM).** People hate it. I hate it. Most savvy Twitter users hate it too.

They're used by spammers, affiliate marketers, and desperate salespeople. Don't be that guy, OK?

Not sure how to set that up? Good. You don't need to know.

Didn't I just specifically ask you NOT to do it? No matter how "cool, valuable, friendly" you think they are—DON'T do it.

This next bit isn't a script, but more of a practice. It's called *engagement*.

Rather than simply pumping out clever tweets and retweeting others, build relationships. My formula for social media success (as a social media enthusiast, remember!) is the **Three R's formula:**

- ✹ **Resources:** Yes, certainly share your blog posts, your micro ideas, and retweets of cool links and thoughts from others. During your first week on Twitter, this is fine. The second week, though, you better get busy with ...

- ✹ **Relationships:** Build relationships with other users you follow, admire, or resonate with. Use public @ messages or private DMs to connect with them, comment on their latest contributions, or thank them for an idea. Be specific. Don't just tweet "@dnewman Hey—Cool!" Instead, tweet this: "@dnewman David, awesome ideas in your book about those social media scripts. Thanks!!!"

- ✹ **Reciprocity:** Once you get the Twitter thing going, you've built some good relationships, and you're seen as a valuable resource and contributor, it's only natural that people will start to promote you with some reciprocal love. They'll respond to your ideas, they'll Retweet you, they'll promote you in their #followfriday recommendations, and they'll scratch your back as you scratch theirs.

That's what puts the "social" into social media, and that's what's going to help you and your business stand out from the crowd!

DO IT! SUCCESS STRATEGY: BE PROGRAMMATIC IN YOUR MARKETING

Mary Foley

When it comes to marketing, especially using social media, goodness knows its ultra easy to get overwhelmed and think, "How am I going to do all this in addition to running the rest of my business?" Here's a solution that's worked for me: Be programmatic. Think *Programming + Automation = You looking like a marketing genius!*

The first step to being programmatic is to decide which social media platforms truly intersect with your target audience. Twitter, Facebook, LinkedIn, Tumblr, Pinterest, and others are not created equal. Pick two or three where your prospects show up and concentrate your energy there.

Second, just like a TV producer, magazine editor, or radio show host, think ahead and pre-program your content. Consider such questions as: What are my key topics or messages? How do these topics logically flow or build from one to the other? Can I create weekly or monthly themes that break down my macro messages into smaller, consumable pieces? What services do I want to feature or what offers can I make?

The value of being programmatic hit home when I co-hosted a weekly radio show, *Girlfriend We Gotta Talk,* for three years. When we first started, our programming approach was, "Whom do we know to interview for next week's show?" Each week it was a time-consuming scramble that always threw off the rest of my schedule. After a while, I'd had enough. As if manna from creative heaven, in a moment of frustration I realized that if we created monthly themes, we could target our focus, search for appropriate guests, and schedule them a month or more in advance. Even more so, we could pre-record a month's worth of shows over two afternoons and then have them aired by the radio station over the following weeks. Why didn't I think of this sooner?

The lesson was not lost on me when I decided it was strategically necessary to take the social media plunge for the rest of my business. I wanted to go from irregular blogging and social media updates to consistently blogging, posting on Facebook, Tweeting, and being active on LinkedIn. My expertise is all about increasing busy women's sanity for their lives and confidence for their careers, all the while having a bit of fun—for myself included! The only way I could attempt to go from zero to 60 mph in 5.7 seconds while maintaining my own sanity was to be programmatic.

First, I decided to use blog articles as my core content in order to showcase my expertise. Then, using social media tools, I set up the process for these blogs to be automatically posted to my Facebook page. Since social media is also about sharing other people's resources, I created a month's worth of third-party links, infographics, or quotes to post on Facebook that supported my message and brand. Each week I offered a "Monday Career Booster," "Wednesday Sanity Check," and "Friday Fun" post. This same content was used to write Tweets and posts on LinkedIn. Once created, the messages were loaded up for automatic posting. If something came up that needed to be added to the mix, it was easy to pop it in.

The beauty of being programmatic is that you create consistent core content for a chunk of time that showcases your expertise, load it up using automation tools, and then you let it happen. At that point, all you have to do is take about 15 minutes a day to check each social media platform, make comments, send personal replies, "like" other people's posts, RT tweets, and truly engage, which is at the heart of cultivating relationships, creating leads, and harvesting a bounty of real-world prospects, customers, and clients.

After setting aside an engineering degree, *Mary Foley* built a 10-year career at AOL during the company's rocky rise to a global brand. Starting as an $8 customer service rep, she was promoted to manager within three years, led a call center of 250, and became the company's first head of corporate training for 12,000 employees.

Today, Mary inspires busy women with practical advice to create sanity in their lives and confidence in their careers—all while having a bit of fun! She is the author of three books, a popular national speaker, and a bodacious get-a-life coach.

Get more ideas and free resources at http://MaryFoley.com.

My marketing coaching client was redoing his web-site. (Can you FEEL his exhilaration?)

He just got his fresh, minty business cards back from the printer. (Can you SMELL those new cards?)

During our next conference call, he asked me, "David, what should go into my e-mail signature file?"

Aha! Trick question.

What followed was my miniseminar, pocket rant, and micro manifesto on **e-mail signature file do's and don'ts.**

After reading this chapter, you will be armed and dangerous in the e-mail signature file combat zone. Suit up, soldier. We're going in HOT!

1. Don't NOT have one. An e-mail signature file is free marketing. If you send 50 e-mails a day, that's 50 marketing opportunities wasted if your e-mails don't have a signature block. You wouldn't go out in public naked, so don't let your e-mails do it either!

2. Don't make it about YOU. "Read my blog, " "Buy my book," "Hire me" are all incredibly juvenile, self-centered, and (frankly) repulsive ways to close an e-mail. This approach is completely devoid of value for the reader, and you're actually *repelling* prospects because you smell desperate and needy.

3. DO include a call to action focused on VALUE. You do want people to take action, but you also want to give them a good reason why. Here's an example from a signature block I've used successfully in the past. Pay attention to the so-what? factor that gives people both the *action* to take—and the *value/benefit* to them:

4. DO include your phone number. The point is real basic, but you'd be amazed at how many business owners and entrepreneurs forget to include their phone number in their e-mail signature block. This is becoming increasingly important as more and more e-mails are now read on mobile devices, primarily smart phones. And some of your prospects, clients, and colleagues simply PREFER the phone. So make it easy for them to reach you that way.

5. DO include a testimonial. **Or three.** You do great work, right? Your clients and customers love you, right? Why not *prove* that point with every e-mail you send out, *especially* prospecting and new client outreach e-mails. My nickname for testimonials is punching people in the face with proof. (My other violent metaphor is content marketing, which is punching people in the face with value. Maybe I should've been a boxer.)

6. Don't feel limited to ONE signature file. Have two or three versions ready to go based on whom you're writing to, what product or service you're writing to them about, and how you'd like to frame your positioning. In my own business, I work with two main types of clients: keynote speaking/seminar clients and marketing coaching/consulting clients. Thus, my **speaking signature file** includes my value prop tagline and three speaking client testimonials. And my **marketing coaching/consulting signature file** has the same contact info but a different value prop statement and an awesome testimonial from one of my consulting clients.

7. DO seduce—DON'T solicit. Here's what doesn't work in an e-mail signature file (or anywhere else in your marketing): brute force solicitation. "Buy my crap" is a pretty lousy marketing message.

Rather, focus on seduction; pull rather than push. Two specific marketing recommendations to make you more seductive (in e-mails and everywhere else too!) are:

- Offer value ("Here's a resource . . . idea ... tool ... article ... recommendation.")
- Invite engagement ("What do you think?" "What's worked for you?" "How can I help?" "Let's discuss this soon.")

Soooo ... (wait for it) ... what do YOU think? What's worked for you? How can I help? Let's discuss this soon. (Seriously, e-mail me at david@doitmarketing.com, and I'd love to see *your* e-mail signature file and answer your marketing questions too!)

And for a ton of FREE marketing resources, guides, and tools to help you market smarter, remember to visit www.doitmarketing.com/book. The "Downloads" section is continually updated with new tools, free bonuses, and special gifts.

31 THE (REAL) IDIOT'S GUIDE TO SOCIAL MEDIA MARKETING

Too many business owners, marketers, and sales professionals want to get involved in social media but sadly do not understand the **intent, ideas, or influence factors** that can make social media such an effective tactic in their overall marketing arsenal.

How can I put this? Ummm ... well, they're IDIOTS.

Relax. IDIOTS is an acronym that stands for the six key misconceptions, faulty assumptions, and pillars of goofy thinking that prevent most thought-leading professionals (YOU perhaps?) from generating maximum results from your social media marketing efforts.

Let's explore these six mistakes and give you some strategies, pointers, and tactics to make sure YOU don't make the same mistakes. Here they are:

> I: "I, Me, My" syndrome
> D: Dumb it down
> I: Information without invitation
> O: Overselling
> T: Talk without action
> S: Short-term focus

Now let's take a look at each of these six mistakes in more detail, as well as how to do social media marketing the right way.

32 I: "I, ME, MY" SYNDROME

No, your social media postings do NOT need to be all about YOU.

In fact, if all you talk about is YOU—your company, your products, your services, your brand, your blog, your resources—people will ignore you, tune you out, and dismiss you for the self-centered IDIOT that you are. (Please remember IDIOT is an acronym; don't take it personally!)

How to do it right: Experts promote other experts. Experts are not insecure about shining the spotlight on others. Experts are curators and pointers-out of cool things.

Experts invite other experts to post guest blogs on their websites, and they, in turn, get invited to do the same! Experts share, collaborate, and cross-promote with other businesses with a genuine abundance mindset, not a scarcity mindset.

> The mantra goes even beyond "give to get"; rather it is "give to give." Do that and social media success is yours.

As long as YOU and YOUR company can be counted on to share interesting, relevant, valuable, sometimes even edgy content, guide your followers to the good stuff online, and position yourself as a reliable guide and sherpa in your area of expertise, you'll get *plenty* of attention, love, and respect. You'll get even MORE if you're not forever focused on hyping only yourself.

Grow up. Step up. Be a real expert, and learn once and for all: It's not about YOU.

Question: When's the last time you promoted a fellow business owner, expert, or thought leader in any of your marketing communications?

DO IT! PROMOTE OTHERS!

Post their guest blog, send out an e-mail featuring their product/service, interview them for your customers and followers, or put their article in your newsletter.

☑ 33 D: DUMB IT DOWN

This mistake comes from your fear that if you give away your VERY BEST ideas, strategies, tools, tactics, insights, and other secret sauce (yes, the very same ideas that go into your products and services and for which you get paid BIG BUCKS from your paying clients), you will somehow **diminish the demand** for those same paid products and services.

So you dumb it down. You post that second-rate article. You remove some detail from that spec sheet because you want people to buy your consulting services, not do it themselves. You post the video that has only three of your 10 key ideas because, heck, if you gave all 10 ideas, they'd never hire you. You've already spilled the candy in the lobby.

Yep, you guessed it: That's IDIOT thinking rearing its ugly head!

HOW TO DO IT RIGHT

The reality is that it works 180 degrees the other way. The ONLY way folks are going to pay you the big bucks is if they have a FIRSTHAND experience of your genius—if they feel it, taste it, touch it, and fully experience it. ONLY THEN will they want more. ONLY THEN will they share it with their colleagues. ONLY THEN will they call their boss over to look at your website or—better still—proactively e-mail your link to another decision maker.

Imagine that **The Rolling Stones** decide that they want to fill their stadium concerts with fans paying $300 per seat so that they can make tens of millions of dollars. And what if they pursue their goal by forbidding radio stations from playing their songs (gasp—letting people listen for FREE). Then they pull their music from online sites like Amazon and iTunes because—gosh—if people can get the very same songs for 99¢, they would never pay $300 to come see it live.

When you put this scarcity thinking in the context of the music industry, you see exactly how ridiculously faulty the argument is!

> **Do you want to be SCARED, or do you want to be SHARED? Your call, but you already know which answer will make you more money (unless you're an IDIOT).**

Question: When's the last time you shared something for free that's so valuable people have paid you good money for it in the course of doing business with you?

DO IT! FREE YOUR VALUE

Take a long hard look at all the great things you give your clients and customers when they buy your product or service.

Now select one item of stand-alone value. And put the mechanism in place to start giving it away. For free. (If you need to grab a brown paper bag because you're starting to hyperventilate, you've chosen the right item.)

An assessment, a sample, a do-it-yourself checklist, a gift—anything that would make a prospect say, "Wow! If they're giving THIS kind of value away for free, imagine how much more we would be if we became a customer!"

✓ 34 I: INFORMATION WITHOUT INVITATION

Social media sites and your blog are not a dumping
ground for your second-rate press releases that you could never even get published in your local paper.

Even rock-solid, current, highly relevant information is **NECESSARY but NOT SUFFICIENT** to fuel your Thought Leadership Platform and build your empire as a smart company.

AN INTERNET SECRET

The Internet actually does **NOT** need more information posted on it. Not from you. Not from me. Not from anyone.

How to do it right: An effective social media campaign will share information of **stand-alone value** and then invite **a two-way (or five-way or 17-way) conversation** about that information. **How? Simple: Ask questions, seek engagement, invite involvement.**

Examples

- On your blog, end each post with the following: "What do YOU think? Use the comments area below and share your experiences or advice on this topic."
- On Facebook, don't pontificate with your posts. Engage your friends with questions such as: "How would you handle ..." or, "Looking for good ideas on ..." or, "Just blogged about Topic X—would love to see a comment from you."
- On Twitter, don't drop fortune cookie rants. Ask QUESTIONS. Simple questions get amazing results. For example: "What's exciting in YOUR world?" "What are you working on right now?" Or even have some fun with fill-in-the-blank tweets like, "Fill in the blank: I'm passionate about _____." To further increase engagement on Twitter, feel free to SELECTIVELY add the request "Please Retweet" so that your engagement question spreads even further. *Note:* Do NOT use this request on more than 5 percent of your tweets; otherwise you'll look sad, desperate, and lonely.

DO IT!
"WHAT DO YOU THINK?"

Offer value, seek opinions, spark conversation—and ask the most powerful question in sales and marketing and leadership and relationships.

Invite a two-way conversation on your blog or through your company's social media accounts by explicitly inviting others to post their ideas, opinions, and feedback.

DO IT! SUCCESS STRATEGY: FOCUS ON YOUR TALK TRIGGERS

Jay Baer

The single most important element of a social media program is making your company worthy of discussion.

We don't tweet meh.

We don't upload blah to Facebook.

We use social media to express feelings that are at the opposing poles of fascination and frustration. So why do so many companies toe the line of average, yet expect customers to shout from the digital rooftops about amazingly mediocre products and services?

If you're going to use social media to accomplish anything of value, you must have a Talk Trigger that rousts your advocates from their naturally drowsy state and gets them typing concise messages of adoration.

But the paradox is that Talk Triggers for social media most often occur offline, not online. The great meal, the over-the-top customer service, the killer swimsuit, the über friendly accountant—all of them manifest in the real world, not in the virtual one.

We use digital to communicate analog. In fact, Keller Fay Group estimates that 91 percent of word of mouth about companies occurs offline; that is, we use social media only to discuss things that REALLY make us want to shout or cry, not the mundane victories and defeats we experience with brands every day.

How do you build a Talk Trigger for your company? There are two options:

Option 1: Spontaneous Talk Triggers

The Talk Triggers that create the most intense advocacy behaviors are those that occur in the wild. These are the moment-in-time occurrences when **a brand dramatically exceeds your (typically low) expectations** in a dramatic way, causing recipients and observers to grab the closest smart phone and post the "you will NOT believe what just happened" messages that put a smile on your face and make you rethink (perhaps subconsciously) the values and merit of the company in question.

A Talk Trigger happened to me when a Southwest Airlines flight attendant made a young boy's day by taping his crayon drawings to the front of the plane and congratulating him publicly. It was one of the warmest, most genuine things I'd ever seen. I live-blogged it (via in-flight Wi-Fi!). Southwest subsequently wrote about my post on their blog and also mentioned it in the in-flight magazine months later.

The flight attendant was also congratulated in the employee podcast.

The spontaneous Talk Trigger was the action of the flight attendant, and it created a lot of chatter and advocacy.

What creates this type of trigger isn't a plan or a spreadsheet, but rather corporate culture. A culture that values being social over doing social. A culture where employees are empowered to work outside the script.

Option 2: Planned Talk Triggers

The other way to create socially fueled advocacy is with planned Talk Triggers. In this case, the brand is **using one or more points of disproportionate awesomeness in a premeditated way to encourage digital statements of support.**

The planned Talk Trigger is, of course, more reliable and can be measured, tested, and optimized. The one thing it cannot be is untrue. If a brand embraces a planned trigger and "nudges" customers to create spread, that trigger better be terrific.

I encountered a fantastic, planned Talk Trigger recently from an outdoor fireplace company called Blue Rooster. I decided to purchase a Blue Rooster fireplace based on reviews, size, and style. It showed up on time, was of higher quality than anticipated, easier to assemble than feared, and worked better than hoped.

But **the best part was the Talk Trigger**. In the parts bag of every Blue Rooster fireplace (I presume) is a marvelous, tiny envelope containing three of the company's business cards. The envelope reads: "Trust us, everyone will ask about your new Blue Rooster Chimney. If you don't feel like talking, just hand them one of these! Call or e-mail us if you need more."

Indeed, several of my friends have asked about it, and I've given away the cards.

It's awfully hard to be great online if you're less than great offline.

What's YOUR Talk Trigger?

Jay Baer is a hype-free, tequila-loving social media and content strategist, speaker, and author. He founded Convince & Convert in 2008. This is the fifth marketing services firm he's started or managed.

Jay has consulted with more than 700 companies on digital marketing since 1994, including Caterpillar, Nike, California Travel & Tourism Commission, Billabong, and 29 of the Fortune 500. He was named one of America's top social media consultants by *Fast Company* magazine, and the Convince and Convert blog is ranked as the world's number one content marketing resource.

He's coauthor of *The NOW Revolution, 7 Shifts to Make Your Business Faster, Smarter, and More Social* (Wiley, 2011), a leading book on social business. An active angel investor, he's also involved in an advisory capacity with several social media and content marketing start-up companies. Connect with Jay at www.ConvinceandConvert.com.

35 O: OVERSELLING

One particularly IDIOTIC business owner bragged
proudly that *all* his social media posts have a hyperlink. Every. Single. One.

Hyperlink to where, you ask?

To his online store, his products, his consulting page, his services overview.

He said, "If you're not linking every post to a selling opportunity, you're just putting a lot of dead-end junk out there, and you'll never make any money."

Now that is pure IDIOT thinking. And the sad news is that it's also the number one complaint that most buyers have about how most business owners and small companies market themselves. It's all self-promotional hype with zero relevance to buyers or their organizations and zero relevance to helping them solve their urgent, pervasive, expensive problems.

Social media is not about posting, "Here's how to buy my crap." It's not about creating an extra dozen or so sales pages for your products, services, or programs.

If your goals are: Sell on Twitter. Sell on Facebook. Sell on LinkedIn. Sell on YouTube ...

Your results will be: Unfollow. Unfriend. Unlink. Unsubscribe. You're done. Buh-bye.

How to do it right: Content comes before commerce. Offer solutions, answers, strategies, templates, tools, and ideas—not sales messages.

Why? Because we're living in an environment of **voluntary attention.** The age of old-school outbound selling (random cold calling, batch-and-blast direct mail, buying ads, and working hard to interrupt strangers) is broken.

The new reality is: **First you earn their attention. THEN you earn their money.**

Action question: How can you turn your next sales message into a value message? How can you solve, fix, advise, and guide instead of hitting your prospects over the head with yet another blunt buy-my-stuff message? And which one do you think they will keep, share, forward, and remember you for?

DO IT! SUCCESS STRATEGY: THREE WAYS TO BE MORE VISIBLE AND CREDIBLE ON SOCIAL MEDIA

Corey Perlman

If you're not generating business with social media, it's just a hobby. Here are three ways to supercharge your efforts.

1. Fish where the fish are. Where are your customers and potential customers spending time online? If they are age 50 and above, the chances are that they are not on Twitter. So I don't suggest you spend a lot of time there! You don't have to be on all social media sites. REPEAT: You don't have to be on all social media sites.

Decide where your audience is spending time, and plant your flag on those sites. If you're typically targeting larger businesses, LinkedIn is probably the place you'll want to spend the most time. If people are using Google to find you or your business, then make sure your Google+ Local Business page is in order by claiming ownership of the page and getting happy customers to review you. More on that in a moment.

2. Be proud of your profiles. When people do online research on you or your business, what's their impression? One thing is for sure: You'll either gain or lose credibility in their eyes. Here are three quick ways to make sure their first impression is a good one:

* Have an attractive, user-friendly website. It's still your most important piece of online real estate. It needs to be nurtured and maintained. It may not win you the business, but it absolutely can lose it for you.

* High numbers—If it's a social media site like a Facebook fan page or LinkedIn profile, nothing says small, unpopular, or old-fashioned more than low numbers. So work on getting lots of fans to your Facebook page, connections to your LinkedIn page, or followers to your Twitter profile. Wherever you decide to have a profile, work on building your numbers.

* Good reviews. There's not much we can do to stop a bad review from happening. It's the web, and people love to use it as a soapbox for their unhappiness. So don't be alarmed if you get one on Google or somewhere else. To protect yourself, be proactive in getting positive reviews. Your champion customers can write them on your Facebook business page, Personal LinkedIn profile, Google+ Local Business page, or somewhere else. Just make sure you ask!

3. Create engaging content. If social media were easy, everyone would be doing it. Wait, everyone is doing it. But very few are doing it well.

What do your prospects and customers deem interesting or valuable? Write about those topics. You'll start to build trust and credibility with your audience.

Then softly promote your business. Mention an event you have coming up, a special that you're running this week, or a customer that you'd like to highlight. These are great ways to softly promote your business instead of aggressively selling.

If you remember nothing else, remember to **make it about them**. I don't care if you're using LinkedIn, Facebook, Twitter, your blog, or something else, think about what your audience cares about and make that the focal point of your pages.

Corey Perlman is an entrepreneur, best-selling author, and nationally recognized social media expert. His most recent book, *eBoot Camp* (Wiley), became an Amazon.com best seller and received global attention with distribution rights deals in both China and India. He delivers keynote presentations and workshops to audiences all over the world.

Corey's company, eBoot Camp, Inc., is a social media marketing company that builds and manages online marketing campaigns for businesses.

Connect with Corey:
www.ebootcamp.com
corey@ebootcamp.com
855-EBOOT-NOW
www.Facebook.com/eBootCamp
www.Linkedin.com/in/coreyperlman
www.Twitter.com/CoreyPerlman

36 T: TALK WITHOUT ACTION

After just now discouraging you from overselling, the next mistake is leaving OUT a vital ingredient to your social media marketing efforts: a call to action (CTA).

Too many business owners, entrepreneurs, and independent professionals do *almost* everything right. Then leave their fans, followers, and subscribers wondering what to do next.

See how many of the following statements sound familiar:

- ✳ "I've been blogging for two years and haven't gotten a single call or e-mail about hiring me."
- ✳ "I work for hours and hours on my e-zine and although I get compliments about how good the articles are, I've never gotten business from it."
- ✳ "I post all the time on Twitter, Facebook, and LinkedIn, but I've never gotten a single phone call from any of my social media efforts."

How to do it right: The answer is simple. People need to be told what to do next. If you want people to e-mail you, explicitly invite them to do so, *and* give them a compelling reason, *and* provide your e-mail address. Example: My friend Scott Ginsberg always ends each blog post with an invitation similar to this one:

> ### SUGGESTION
>
> **For a list called "9 Things Every Writer Needs to Do Every Day," send an e-mail to me, and you win the list for free!**
>
> *Scott Ginsberg*
> *That Guy with the Nametag*
> **Author, Speaker, Publisher, Artist, Mentor**
> scott@hellomynameisscott.com

If you want people to call you, use the same strategy. Invite the call, and provide your phone number. For example, Gerard Braud is a media training and crisis communications expert who introduces himself to hand-selected high-probability prospects on LinkedIn and ends his message this way:

> *If a brief conversation about your team's media-readiness and/or crisis communication plans would be valuable, please call me or drop me a line.*
>
> *Wishing you continued success,*
> *Gerard Braud (Jared Bro) Tel: 985-624-9976*

Action question: Are you using value-first CTAs in your e-mails, blogs, and social media postings? Are you giving people a compelling reason to engage further with you in meaningful ways, such as subscribing to your e-zine, calling you, or e-mailing you?

✓ **37** S: SHORT-TERM FOCUS

The final mistake is to think of social media in the same way that you might think of outbound sales activity.

Think about it:

- ✻ Cold calls, e-mail blasts, direct mail—for those things, the natural question to ask is, "OK, how much did we SELL TODAY?"
- ✻ **You made 100 dials,** you connected with 20 humans, you had 14 conversations, you qualified five serious prospects. "How much did you SELL TODAY?"
- ✻ **You sent 10,000 postcards.** Requests came back for 300 quotes. "How many widgets did you SELL TODAY?"

Social media marketing doesn't work that way. Social media is, well, social. It's about relationships and trust. Relationships and trust don't have an on/off switch; they develop over time.

Transactions happen today from relationships you built last week, last month, and last year. The benefit of that—and the reason it's worth the wait—is that social media gives you a permanent asset: trust.

How to do it right: Blog entries are forever. They continue to sell your expertise, your company, and your value day after day, week after week, year after year. **LinkedIn recommendations are forever.** People who wrote glowingly of you in 2002 are still selling for you and your reputation today.

A voice mail? BEEP—gone. An e-mail? ZAP—gone. A face-to-face meeting? DONE—bye. **Those all happen today, and they're gone today.**

Sure, you have to sell today. You have to make your quota today. You have to feed your family today. But social media marketing helps you ensure that what you create ONCE today works and lasts and brings customers and clients to you for many years to come.

Not because you SOLD them like an IDIOT, but because you built the trust and relationships that HELPED THEM BUY **today, tomorrow, and beyond**!

Action question: What *permanent assets* are you building today so that your best-fit buyers will seek you out for your expertise, ideas, and solutions at the precise moment they are ready to spend money on what you sell? Are you putting *irresistible bait* on *enough hooks* in the *right ponds* so that you won't go hungry next week, next month, and next year?

DO IT! SUCCESS STRATEGY: 12 TIPS TO BECOMING SUCCESSFUL ON LINKEDIN

Viveka Von Rosen

1. Treat your LinkedIn profile like a website.

Make sure it is formatted, clean, and free of spelling and grammatical errors. There is nothing worse than trying to represent yourself as a professional and have the word proffessional spelled incorrectly! (Did you catch that? Did it make you cringe?)

I have a LinkedIn profile questionnaire that I give my clients (you can download it at www.linkedin.com/in/linkedinexpert in the Box.net app). Use either my questionnaire or a Word (Pages) doc in order to catch spelling and grammar issues.

You will also get a better idea of what your profile will look like on the LinkedIn website. In some sections of LinkedIn you can also copy in bullets and special characters. (Use "Insert symbol" to get special characters) Alas—still no bolding or italics other than what LinkedIn itself formats in your profile. Your Company Profile now has more options in the Product and Service section.

Another bonus, if you've already created your profile in a Word document, sections of it can easily be copied into other social media platforms to keep your branding unified.

2. Know your keywords.

Like any website, LinkedIn's internal search engines weigh your keywords heavily in its searches. Make sure you place your most important search or keywords and keyword phrases strategically throughout your profile. Some places you might want to consider are your:

- Professional headline (120 characters)
- Title fields (100 characters)

- Specialties (500 characters, if available)
- Interests (1,000 characters)
- Recommendations
- Education (activities and societies)

3. Keep your name clean.

Put only your first name in the first name field and your last name in the last name field. If someone is searching for you by name, LinkedIn will have a hard time finding you if your last name looks like this: "Smith, PhD. John A. (johnsmith@gmail.com) LION 941-555-1555."

Not only that, but it goes against LinkedIn's End User Agreement to have anything other than your name in the name field. That is what got my profile blacklisted (i.e., unfindable under my keywords), resulting in my losing thousands of dollars worth of work. Learn from my mistakes!

4. Keep your photo professional.

I recommend a close-up and a smile. A full body shot of you and your family, you and your car, you and that fish you caught last week is unclear and unprofessional.

I have seen some artists use artistic renderings of themselves, which is clever if your image is still clear. LinkedIn doesn't like logos. The End User Agreement states that if you are going to post a picture, it must be your likeness.

5. Don't ignore the post-an-update function.

LinkedIn's update function is much more robust than it used to be (taking some tips from Facebook and Twitter).

People can now like, share, and comment on your updates, which helps to build relationships within LinkedIn. You can also see people's activity, so that, like Twitter, you can get a better idea of what really interests them and what they invest their time in.

With the introduction of LinkedIn Signal, the update section can now be a functional part of your SME (subject matter expertise) and content strategy. Make sure you take a little time each day to "like" and "comment" on the updates of your network as well.

Finally, make sure you use Signal to monitor your own brand, your clients, and your competitors.

6. Personalize your public profile URL.

Make sure your public profile reflects your name, your business, or your area of expertise: for example, www.linkedin.com/in/linkedinexpert.

Nothing says, "I'm a LinkedIn neophyte" like a public profile that reads: http://linkedin.com/pub/firstname-lastname9890734-akjshfiho.

7. Personalize your websites.

When you edit your website, the drop-down menu gives you the option of "Other." By clicking on that, a new field opens up that allows you to type in your business name, website name, call to action, or description of your website. So instead of "Company Website" or "Personal Website," this section can read "Social Media for Women" or "Click here: IP Legal Advice"

8. Juice up your "Experience" section.

"Experience" is not your resume. Make sure the jobs you choose to list support each other. Be sure to put all your keywords in the title section.

Use the 1,000 characters in the "Experience" description section to tell people why they should hire you or your company or buy your product. Tell a save-the-day story. Put in a testimonial.

"Experience" is a great place to list wins, different companies you have helped, seminars or workshops you have presented, a minishot of your personal website. Use this section as the foundation for your Company Profile.

9. List your "Additional Education."

Make sure you list your certifications and licenses as well as traditional education. LinkedIn has now added new sections where you can list areas of expertise, publications, patents, licenses, and certifications.

10. Get recommendations.

Even though you no longer need three recommendations to have a complete profile (according to LinkedIn), I suggest getting between 10 and 15.

When you are asking for recommendations, provide a bulleted list of your skills, strengths, and services so that people will write a more complete recommendation and not, "She's nice."

You might want to add some of the better recommendations to your website. Ask for recommendations from thought leaders in your field, former colleagues, and well-known clients.

To see some great recommendations, check out Howard Lewinter's profile at www.linkedin.com/in/howardlewinter.

11. Use the applications.

Every day, LinkedIn is adding more useful applications. You can embed up to eight in your profile. See which ones will be most useful to you. I recommend their blogging apps (either Blog Link or WordPress), Box.net, Slideshare, Behance (to show YouTube Videos), Legal Updates and JD Supra if you are a lawyer, and Amazon Reading List, especially if you are an author.

12. Always be courteous and give more than you get.

LinkedIn is a business networking site. Be courteous. Try to answer Inmails, messages, and requests for introductions within 72 hours. Remember your "Please" and "Thank you." Help someone out.

LinkedIn is a great place to get information, to get connections, to get clients, to get employees. But follow the golden rule: "Do unto others as you would have them do unto you." Don't spam. Don't infiltrate e-mail boxes with constant sales messages. Instead, share valuable information via your groups, updates, and answers, and let clients come to you.

Viveka Von Rosen is known internationally as the LinkedIn Expert and speaks to business owners, corporations, law firms, and professional associations on the benefits of marketing with social media, particularly LinkedIn.

She is the author of *LinkedIn Marketing: An Hour a Day* (Wiley), and she is also a regular source on LinkedIn for prestigious news outlets, such as Mashable.com, SocialMediaExaminer.com, and *The Miami Herald*. She is the host of the biggest LinkedIn chat on Twitter: #LinkedInChat (recently quoted by Mashable as one of the top 10 business blogs) and co-moderator of LinkedStrategies, the largest LinkedIn strategy group on LinkedIn. She is constantly learning, sharing, and transferring social media skills and strategies to her tribe.

Viveka has more than 22,000 first-level connections and a network of over 23 million people on LinkedIn, and over 44,000 followers on Twitter. Her seminars, webinars, and workshops have taught and trained well over 10,000 people. Connect with Viveka at http://linkedintobusiness.com.

PART SIX

THE "S" WORD

38 SELL LIKE A GIRL

What can a 12-year-old teach you about sales?

Quite a bit, as it turns out.

It's Girl Scout Cookie time in our part of the world. For those of you who are unfamiliar with the sights, tastes, and overall experience of helping your daughters sell Thin Mints, Samoas, and Do-Si-Dos, you're missing a fundamental and wide-ranging education about the dynamics of sales, selling, and salespeople.

Here are some points I've garnered while helping my daughter, Becca (a loyal member of Girl Scout Troop 3129) make her sales numbers for three years running when she was between the ages of 10 and 12. These pointers are hard earned, field tested, and as applicable to you and your business as they were to Becca and hers.

1. **It's who you know.** It's true: The cookie business is a relationship business. Our next-door neighbor bought nine boxes—bam! Neighbors on the other side bought two boxes, then three, then still more. Why? Because Becca had something to sell. What's your personal brand doing these days? If you switched products, services, or companies, would people buy from you just because it's YOU?

2. **It's not about the product.** It's time to get the lawyers upset. Ready? Girl Scout cookies, for the most part, taste terrible. (Thin Mints are the one exception, in my humble opinion.) And they have enough fat, calories, and cholesterol in them to power a small Japanese alternative-fuel vehicle. You want good cookies? Buy Oreos, Mallomars, Ginger Snaps, Nutter Butters, Grasshoppers, Deluxe Grahams, Fudge Sticks, etc. Yet Girl Scout Cookies

sell like crazy, year after year, bringing millions to the bottom line of Girl Scouts of the USA.

3. **It's not about price.** At the time of this writing, Girl Scout cookies cost $4 a box. The smallest box, by weight, is 7 ounces, and the largest is 10 ounces. The small size of most retail cookies is about 12 ounces and costs about $2.79. Girl Scout cookies give even premium brands, such as Pepperidge Farm, a run for their money when it comes to high cost. Did I mention one of our neighbors bought nine boxes at a clip?

4. **It's not about need.** Face it, nobody needs Girl Scout cookies. For example, the girls were out doing a "Cookie Shop" at a local hardware store. (Local merchants, malls, and grocery stores allow Girl Scouts to set up a table for sales on their premises to support the cause.) The number one objection we heard was, "I already have some Girl Scout Cookies at home—more than I need!" So why did they buy? Because they had a relationship with their salesperson that was more important than their need, desire, or use for the actual product. Did you know that Girl Scout cookies make great gifts, freeze really well, and are sold for only a short time every year? Can you learn from this and apply the lesson to YOUR sales message?

5. **It's not about competition; it's all about contacts and referrals.** So who is selling to all those customers who have more Girl Scout cookies at home than they need? Naturally, it's **their** Girl Scout. What are the chances of Becca selling a box of cookies to someone whose daughter is also selling the same cookies for the same price? You got it: less than zero. Is Becca going to bang her head against the wall bemoaning those lost sales? Of course not. She tapped into her network of networks: neighbors, cousins, kids, and parents at the Y where she plays basketball, my former colleagues at my old job who have become good family friends (and Becca's customers in previous years). Do you know how to fill your pipeline when things seem dry? Do you know how to move your prospects along to becoming customers, satisfied customers, and then customers for life—not of the product or service you're selling today, but of YOU and what-

ever value proposition you might be offering now and in the future?

6. **When times are tough and things look quiet, that's the time to push harder than ever.** Cookie sales end at a certain time each year. When the sale is two weeks away from the ending date, Girl Scout Cookies are being sold everywhere you look. We probably had 10 to 12 boxes left over by the time the deadline came each year. Was Becca depressed that we didn't meet our goal? Were we failures as salespeople? Only if we had quit when it ended. You see, as soon as everyone else stops selling, stops marketing, and stops running the Cookie Shops, these cookies move up from a commodity to a valuable asset. It's the same thing in your business: When the market is down, your competition has pulled their ads; they think it's time to hunker down, get back to basics, and cut, cut, cut! However, that's the worst time to cut; you have everyone's attention! There's actually much less noise out there for your message to compete against. Push now, and you'll be heard!

WHAT DOES THIS MEAN TO YOU AND YOUR BUSINESS?

It's simple: Now is the time to get back in the saddle and ride your sales and marketing activities harder than ever. You've got the floor. You've got more relationships and more people rooting for you than you realize, and if you cut through the old excuses about your product, price, competition, the economy, and all the rest of it, you'll see the sales breakthroughs that lie ahead. **Why waste another minute?**

39 YOUR SALES TO-DON'T LIST

This list of 10 one-liners comes from an old *Purchasing* magazine survey. In an ironic twist, *Purchasing* magazine, founded in 1915, ceased publication in April 2010. Apparently, not enough people were purchasing *Purchasing*!

I've expanded on each survey item with my comments and suggestions for you and your business.

TOP 10 THINGS SALESPEOPLE DO THAT BUYERS DISLIKE

10. Failure to keep promises

Two suggestions here:

1. OVERpromise and OVERdeliver.
2. Learn to shut up.

When you say, "I'll do my best to get it here Tuesday," your customer hears, "I promise it'll be here Tuesday."

In fact, even if you say, "I can't promise it'll be here Tuesday," some customers will *still* hear, "I promise it'll be here Tuesday." It's better NOT to say anything than to be perceived as someone who breaks promises!

9. Lack of creativity

Sales author and Hall of Fame speaker Jeffrey Gitomer says this about the role of creativity in sales:

* Where does creativity come from? You learn it.
* How important is creativity in sales success? VERY!

* How creative are you? Not very.
* Can you improve your creativity? Yes!

Case closed. Want some ideas to get you started?

Download your free "Resource List: Great Books for Marketing and Sales Professionals," plus over 100 marketing tools, templates, and bonuses from **http://www.doitmarketing.com/book.**

8. Failure to make and keep appointments

Failure to make 'em: Do you seriously think your prospect has time to chat when you decide to just drop by because you're in the neighborhood?

Failure to keep 'em: That's right. You've got a precious hard-earned appointment. Go ahead—blow it off. Who cares? It's just money.

7. Lack of awareness of the customer's operation

"What do you guys do here anyway?" How could YOU not know? Research is the key. Do research on the web, talk to people at the company or in the industry, make some calls, get the lay of the land. You'll stand head and shoulders above the crowd.

6. Taking the customer for granted

The Forum Corporation did a study of commercial customers that were lost by 14 major manufacturing and service companies. Here's what they found:

* 15 percent of those customers found a better product.
* 15 percent found a cheaper product.
* 20 percent left because of a "lack of contact and individual attention" from the supplier.
* 49 percent left because "contact from supplier's personnel was poor in quality."

Those last two numbers should be a real wake-up call. What do they say? They say this: "My salesperson or account manager sucks." Plain and simple. Turns out that clients don't leave suppliers; they leave salespeople!

The era of "I just close 'em; someone else babysits 'em." is over. In fact, it's so old, it's starting to stink.

What would it mean to your business if you could prevent 69 percent of your current customer attrition? Well, YOU can!

5. Lack of follow-through

This one is simple: Do what you say, and say what you do.

Need more detail? OK. The first part of this involves keeping your promises. See number 10 above.

But the second part is equally, if not more, important. Many salespeople do a great job for their clients, and the clients never know it. Why? Because the salespeople don't have time to close the loop and TELL the client what they're doing to help them or resolve their problem. Salespeople think, "I'm taking care of it," or, "I'll let the client know once everything is finished."

Meanwhile, hours or days or weeks go by. If all clients hear is a whole lotta nuthin', then that's also what they think you're doing! All it takes is a simple phone call or e-mail to keep them updated on exactly what's being done on their behalf, the expected timetable, and how the process works ("I'll e-mail you the forms Monday, and then as soon as you fax them back to me, I'll submit them. Then I'll call you Wednesday with an update either way.")

To be good at follow-through, you need to be good at *communicating* about follow-through!

4. Lack of product knowledge

This one is simple too. Shame on you. If you don't know your own products/services inside and out, why should customers buy from you?

Order takers don't need product knowledge (actually, that's not quite true either!) but sales professionals definitely do. How do you get it?

* Ask!
* Research.
* Host a customer lunch, and find out what your product/service means to your current clients and how they're using it.
* Study your industry association's research and training resources.

✳ Hang out with one of your larger customers for a day, and see for yourself how they use, live with, and benefit from your product or service.

3. Overaggressiveness and failure to listen

Are you talking to me? Are YOU talking to ME?

The age of what I call jerk selling is over. People don't buy from jerks. They used to—back when there wasn't much choice—but not anymore.

Overaggressiveness comes from desperation.

Big turnoff.

Failure to listen comes from being a egocentric jerk.

Bigger turnoff.

Guess what, Jerky. It's NOT all about you. It's all about the customer, and the best skill (not TOOL or TECHNIQUE, but real SELLING SKILL) you can develop is genuine curiosity and authentic listening. This isn't something you can pick up in a one-day seminar. It takes time, attention, practice, and reinforcement.

You know why some salespeople—even some who have had a lot of sales training—still have trouble closing? They don't keep the sale open long enough to listen deeply and establish the value of their solution in their prospects' eyes.

Closing problems are relationship problems and listening problems.

2. Lack of interest or purpose ("Just checking in")

Purpose is critically important to every step of the sales process. It starts small, such as asking, "What's the purpose of this next call I'm about to make?" But I take it much further in our Do It! Marketing seminars—all the way up to the largest and most meaningful purpose you have professionally ("What is my work?" "Why does our company exist?") and personally ("Who is my self?" "Why am I here?")

Do you think this is woo-woo nonsense?

LensCrafters doesn't. And they're one of the world's most successful and profitable sales organizations. Here is LensCrafters' statement of purpose: **"We will be the best at helping the world see."**

They then outline the concrete meaning of their purpose statement:

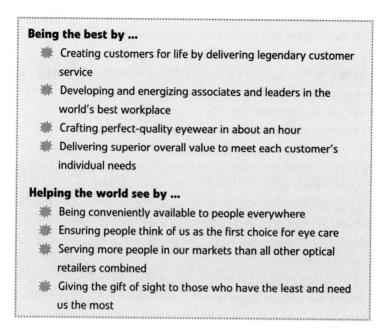

Being the best by ...

- 🌟 Creating customers for life by delivering legendary customer service
- 🌟 Developing and energizing associates and leaders in the world's best workplace
- 🌟 Crafting perfect-quality eyewear in about an hour
- 🌟 Delivering superior overall value to meet each customer's individual needs

Helping the world see by ...

- 🌟 Being conveniently available to people everywhere
- 🌟 Ensuring people think of us as the first choice for eye care
- 🌟 Serving more people in our markets than all other optical retailers combined
- 🌟 Giving the gift of sight to those who have the least and need us the most

So each LensCrafters manager (who works in a store at a mall, remember) wakes up each morning with the goal of "helping the world see," whereas the competition goes to work to sell more eyeglasses.

Which one would get YOU more jazzed?

And their charitable activities in the third world ("The Gift of Sight" program started in 1988) is also a fabulous motivator and a point of pride within the company's ranks.

They must be doing something right. LensCrafters is hugely profitable and has consistently maintained a spot on Fortune's 100 Best Companies to Work For list for the last several years.

1. Lack of preparation

It's amazing how many salespeople pick up the phone, or walk into a meeting, or sit down for lunch with a prospect, and simply wing it.

Every other professional is expected (or required to) prepare, practice, and think of every possible outcome and its corresponding response: surgeons, lawyers, football players, combat soldiers, airline pilots, electricians, paramedics, and engineers.

Also, remember point 7, and think of it this way: How can you NOT prepare?

A good preparation exercise is called Missile/Defense. On the left side of a piece of paper, write down every potential question, problem, or objection that you might encounter. These are the sales missiles.

On the right side, write down your supporting research, value proposition, benefit, testimonial, or success story. These are your defenses.

By the way, this is not about defending your sale in the traditional sense. In fact, I'm totally against a lot of the adversarial language and thinking that is popular in some sales training about "us versus them" and "salespeople versus prospects" and "playing by their rules versus your rules." To me, that's a lot of nonsense. If your prospects are your enemies, you don't deserve their business.

This preparation exercise is more about the process of thinking about and writing out where your prospect's needs intersect with your products and services. It's about finding common ground, where it makes overwhelming sense for the prospect to do business with you.

Only you can do that work. And that work is called preparation!

Download your own copy of the Missile/Defense sales worksheet at **www.doitmarketing.com/book**.

DO IT! SUCCESS STRATEGY: SIX RULES FOR SELLING TO THE C-SUITE

Mark Hunter, "The Sales Hunter"

The C-suite—the domain of the CEO, COO, and other senior company personnel—can unlock huge opportunities if you handle things correctly, but the rules are different than in most other selling situations.

1. It's about outcomes, not price. If the outcome is what the C-suite member wants, then price is irrelevant. If you do mention price, you will find yourself being ushered to the purchasing department faster than you can say "Oops." The questions you ask and the information you share need to be focused on the issues your customers are facing, not on what you think they might like or want to hear. If you build your sales plan around helping your customers achieve outcomes in which they will find value, you'll more likely have a meaningful meeting.

2. It is all about trust. People at this level place a high degree of value in the opinions of others they trust. Until there is a level of trust between you and the C-suite member, you can count on getting very little done.

3. It is all about time. These people are busy. Respect their time and know they develop opinions fast and make decisions even faster. Start on time, end on time, and, most of all, make each minute you have with them valuable for them. As much as you and I might feel we're pressed for time, the person in the C-suite is working at a pace 10 times faster than we are. Even if you have 30 minutes scheduled for a meeting, you don't necessarily have to take the full 30 minutes. Work the agenda, not the clock. And remember that, in no case, should you exceed the allotted time.

4. Don't talk specifics. Talk strategic. If you walk into a C-suite office and start talking about specific product features and detailed information, you are talking about things the C-suite person neither cares about nor has an interest in. People at this level look at the big picture. They're strategic thinkers. Talk in strategic terms.

5. Watch out for influencers. In every company, there are people outside the C-suite who are looking to get into the C-suite, and they'll do whatever it takes. These people will crush a vendor if it can help them achieve their objective. The same goes for others in an organization who may not want to be part of the C-suite but who want to make sure their opinion is heard by the C-suite. Again, these people can come out of nowhere, and in a single meeting, they can do incredible damage to your proposal.

6. Every C-Suite has a gatekeeper. Treat the gatekeeper as you would the buyer. Gatekeepers go by a wide number of names, such as administrative assistant, executive assistant, director, or manager. Many times they aren't physically located in the C-suite area of a company, but they're still gatekeepers. These people control the calendar and they often even control the overall thinking of the C-suite. Treat the gatekeeper in the same manner you would the person with whom you want to meet. The questions you ask the gatekeeper are going to determine whether you can actually meet with the person in the C-suite.

Selling to the C-Suite does not have to be treacherous or overly difficult. In fact, it actually can be quite lucrative and productive—if you follow these six rules.

Mark Hunter, The Sales Hunter, is author of *High-Profit Selling: Win the Sale Without Compromising on Price*. He is a consultative selling expert committed to helping individuals and companies identify better prospects and close more profitable sales. To read his blog and receive a weekly sales tip, visit www.TheSalesHunter.com.

✓ 40 YOU DON'T NEED SALES TRAINING

If you're a business owner, entrepreneur, or independent professional, you probably have asked yourself some or all of the following questions:

* How can I get more customers and clients?
* How can I get better customers?
* How do I sell more to the clients I've got?
* Can I earn more money and still have a life?
* Why are sales activities so difficult sometimes?
* Is there a "right" way to sell?
* Where can I turn for hands-on advice when I need it?
* When will this get easier?

Here's what most sales training companies will tell you is the answer to your business growth challenges: **sales training**.

Here's what most marketing consultants will tell you is your answer: **marketing consulting.**

Well, neither is the case.

If anything, you need to UNlearn what a lot of sales training and marketing seminars and sales books have told you. You need to reconnect with how to sell based on WHO you are—in short, to start using and recognizing the power of selling differently.

And here's something new and different coming from someone like me: You don't need to hire anybody.

Sales training (and any training) is for people who lack knowledge.

My clients are typically very smart. But they've learned to sell from the head, using gimmicks, clever phrases, manipulative closing techniques, and artificial rapport building. None of this works or lasts because it's outside-in, trying to force you into a mold that you just don't fit.

A truly effective approach will unlock your thinking and help you sell for real.

It's more authentic, and it works and lasts because you start to sell from the inside-out, based on WHO you are, not on an external set of behaviors that work for only a very small percentage of old-school salespeople.

Think about it. You know how to sell (or at least you know you don't like what a lot of sales training SAYS is the way to sell).

You have probably had some sales training, and you might have gone to a few sales seminars. You have probably read a sales or marketing book or two, and you may even have heard some fluffy woo-woo talks that call themselves sales training. However, none of it stuck because none of it seemed relevant to YOU or spoke to your desire to help people by providing genuine value.

> **You need a personal sales strategy that seamlessly combines your natural self with your strongest message to your best prospects with the highest value, using the least time and effort.**

Then you need a plan and an accountability mechanism (sales manager, coach, or colleague) who will help you work your plan, day by day, prospect by prospect.

Unlike traditional sales training, true sales effectiveness is a process, not an event. And it always works from the INSIDE out. That means that it's focused on internal skills and lasting tools, not on sales training gimmicks or external techniques.

When selecting a professional to help boost your sales, you need to be aware that a lot of marketing consultants give **detailed blueprints but no tools**. And a lot of sales training provides **specific tools but no overall strategy**.

You want to look for a resource that integrates big-picture marketing strategy with day-to-day selling tools so that your selling WORKS and so that MORE SALES HAPPEN.

The truth is that nobody needs one-size-fits-all sales training or here's-your-marketing-plan-good-luck consulting. You simply need a customized set of keys to unlock the business answers you need. There is no cookie cutter. You're no cookie.

So skip the sales training and keep reading this book, especially the **21-Day Marketing Launch Plan** that you'll find at the end of this book to give you the day-to-day tactical guidance you need. And grab all the instant-action resources, tools, and templates waiting for you online at **www.doitmarketing.com/book**.

PART SEVEN

GET BETTER LEADS

☑ 41 MARKET TO PEOPLE WHO ARE ALREADY LISTENING

Are you marketing to people who are already listening?

It is very, very hard to market your products and services to everyone. And, frankly, not everyone needs or wants what you're offering. That's just hard reality.

But there is a core demographic that is already tuned in. They don't need convincing. They're just waiting to hear from you about what's new, what you're up to, and how you can help them.

Aren't those people worth reaching out to?

Of course, they are!

Do you know who they are and how to reach them?

Hmmm. Let's think about that one.

You could—and should—start with your company's existing customers. These are your most valuable prospects. They convert the quickest, and they are also the most profitable—not to mention that they are the least expensive to find and engage with!

You could create an e-mail list. You could integrate Tell-a-Friend forwarding into your e-mails and web pages. You could offer referral bonuses of exclusive services or benefits. You could develop your existing fans into enthusiastic brand advocates and multiply your sales and marketing effectiveness by 10 or 20 times.

You could host events like "Welcome-to-the-Neighborhood" Breakfasts or Customer Roundtables.

You could create an award like Community Hero or Entrepreneur of the Year. In short, you could (and should) **make a big business splash in a small business pond.**

☑ **42** WHY YOU *DON'T* WANT TO BE IN THE BOOK

In my role as a marketing speaker and marketing coach, my clients and audience members often ask me if they should spend the time and money to be listed in this directory or that trade show book or some magazine's Marketplace section.

You're about to get the answer for YOU and YOUR business if you've ever wondered the same thing.

But first, remember the *Yellow Pages*?

Their old tagline was, "Let Your Fingers Do the Walking."

It was more convenient—in the 1960s and 1970s—to use the *Yellow Pages* and your rotary phone to find out what you needed to know about local businesses than to literally walk from store to store or from office to office.

In fact, when you walked around town, it was common to see window stickers that proudly proclaimed things like "Find Tony's One-Hour Cleaners in the *Yellow Pages*." (Did you really need to look them up in the *Yellow Pages* when you are right there physically in front of their store?)

Yes, you could find Tony's One-Hour Cleaners in the *Yellow Pages*–along with Sam's One-Hour Cleaners, Jiffy Dry Cleaning, and dozens of other competitors all over town. This was great for consumers up until about 1992 when the web took over much of this same functionality and multiplied its marketing power.

But today, buying ads in any directory is pretty dumb.

Why? Because the moment you're in the book, you're a commodity. You are *actively* inviting your prospects, customers, clients, and influencers to comparison shop your ad versus their ad, your listing versus their listing, your trade show booth versus their trade show booth.

And don't get me started on trade show exhibiting. Unless you're in the top 5 percent of folks who truly know what they're doing, exhibiting at a trade show is nothing more than endless days of exhaustion and massive expense, only to be proactively ignored by people walking rapidly to the back of the exhibit center to get their bagel while working insanely hard to avoid eye contact with you and your staff at all costs.

As I share in my Do It! Marketing keynotes and seminars, we're living in an *attention* economy. First, you must earn your prospect's attention. Only then do you get the chance to earn their money.

And these days, it's hard to earn anyone's attention with a BIGGER ad, a BOLDER directory listing, or a SPLASHIER banner.

Nobody cares. Truly. So give it up.

The expiration date on that strategy has come and gone like a bucket of old yogurt.

Today, you can save all that money and put it toward creating resources, tools, and content that your target market will VALUE, will KEEP, and will SHARE.

✓ **43** OLD MEDIA IS DEAD! LONG LIVE OLD MEDIA!

According to a headline in *BtoB Magazine*: "Forecast: Internet will be the only medium to grow ad dollars this year." (The year doesn't matter; it's been the same story every year since 2009!)

Of course, Internet and mobile ad dollars will grow. It's just too bad that most traditional media ad execs stubbornly refuse to see the light.

A great example came across my desk from an old media (print) publisher friend of mine in response to one of my articles titled, "Old Media Is Dead—Welcome to the Age of Inbound Marketing." Here is his email verbatim plus a ton of free sand into which he firmly sticks his head:

There's a reason they call Google a search engine ... users have an immediate need to find information and Google becomes the handy reference. If that need doesn't exist for any length of time, the user isn't compelled to go to that search engine (or for that matter, any other website). I'm not trying to minimize Google's value, just keeping it all in perspective.

Furthermore, most users don't want spam (read "advertising") to be visible . . . they find it an intrusion to see a message pop up when not requested. How many iPods do you think Apple would have sold strictly by posting a link/ad on Google ads? Do you think they could have approached the 1mm plus goal? Do you think their heavy TV campaign was a useless expenditure? Why not just use their own website? Do you know something the good folks at Apple don't?

I can tell you my 17-year-old son certainly doesn't want me to mute the TV when their ads are running. The point is that the Internet is a valuable addition to the "traditional" media mix but certainly not its replacement.

This is classic "say-it-isn't-so" wishful thinking. This poor sap's print advertising clients are NOT Fortune 500 companies (like Apple) that can afford to do a wide range of brand and image advertising. They are much more direct response marketers; they want the phone to ring and the orders to come in when they spend dollars on his ads. And with the possible exception of laser-targeted industry-specific publications (for example, one great way to reach financial advisors is through *Advisor Today*), putting marketing dollars into old media isn't going to do it!

Can he be serious when he expands his Apple-TV-commercials-are-cool argument to suggest that all kinds of people WANT to watch all kinds of TV commercials, and thus Advertising 1.0 is alive and well?

That's not only stupid, it's being irresponsible with client marketing dollars. My point is that you can't fix stupid.

Some marketing and media execs "get it" that their world has changed dramatically. While some other marketers (and business owners and entrepreneurs) are happy to rearrange deck chairs on the *Titanic* and slowly sink under the waves as the orchestra plays on.

PS: And be extra thankful you're not running a clueless print media company that's hoping Google will just go away. Sad, isn't it?

☑ 44 NOBODY IS GOING TO STEAL YOUR IDEA

A lot of entrepreneurs and businesspeople come up with marketing ideas, product ideas, or service ideas and say, "Wow—that's really terrific. Only one problem—what if someone steals my idea?"

My standard answer: Nobody can steal YOUR idea. When they do, it becomes *their* idea and, from that moment on, it starts to diverge from what you would do, how you would do it, and the value you would bring to it.

Mark Moskowitz, the writer and producer of the movie *Stone Reader*, once told me: "I used to be worried that everybody I pitched my stories to in Hollywood would steal them. And once or twice that happened. But you know what? I would have never gotten this movie made if I hadn't told *everybody* about it."

A client of mine put it another way: "David, I used to be afraid of telling people what I do. Now, I'm afraid *not to.*"

What gives your work its edge is the simple fact that **you've spent years percolating your ideas.**

Perhaps you've done so unwittingly, or subconsciously, or unintentionally, but that doesn't matter.

The ideas ARE yours, and you know them better than anyone.

There's some mighty leverage in that.

For free tools to *Develop Your Elevator Pitch and Develop Your Positioning Statement*—along with 100 other marketing resources plus your **21-Day Do It! Marketing Playbook**—visit **www.doitmarketing.com/book.**

DO IT! SUCCESS STRATEGY: SIX WAYS TO GENERATE SALES

Melinda F. Emerson

Although sales are essential to your business success, many small business owners focus on lead generation only when they are in panic mode. Don't get so busy with your day-to-day operations that you forget to focus on your ongoing marketing activities. To help you reach your sales goals, here are six marketing techniques to make sure you always have a rich pipeline of prospective customers and clients ready to do business with you.

1. Profile your best customers. Who are your most valuable and profitable customers? How much do they spend with you annually? You must understand what value your business brings to your customers so that you can continue fulfilling their needs. Business issues can change quickly, making vendors potentially interchangeable. Be sure to thank your customers too; no one owes you their business.

2. Talk with your clients. You must stay on top of the needs of your customers and understand any new factors that influence their industry or their decision-making processes. Have 10 questions to ask, and then make sure you engage them around some personal small talk: kids, vacations, holiday plans, and the like. The more personal the relationship, the more that relationship will allow you to obtain critical information and create a strong advocate for your company.

3. Align marketing efforts with your sales goals. Sales and marketing have to work together in a small business. Plan your marketing programs based on the number of sales leads you need to generate. If you know you need 500 leads per month in order to close 50 sales, then determine how many phone calls, e-mails, blog posts, Facebook ads, and Twitter messages must be made, sent, or posted per month to drive the desired traffic. You must establish a sales process and then proactively work your marketing efforts so that they generate the sales results.

4. Never take your eye off the competition. Identify several competitors. Discover what benefits they provide to their customers. Use their websites to gain insights. Compare your branding, value proposition, and pricing. Based on your assessment, develop at least three strategies that you will use to position yourself effectively against them.

5. Refine your elevator pitch. As a small business owner, your most important job is selling yourself and your business. Being able to succinctly explain your business builds trust, but you shouldn't use the same pitch forever. From time to time, switch it up a little. Add a brief client list; mention a recent award or media hit. Elevator pitches are designed to draw in your target and keep the dialogue going. Offer just enough to get the prospect to start asking questions.

6. Use a vision board. All businesses have ups and downs. How you get through the tough days in your business makes a big difference in your productivity. I advise all my small business clients to develop a vision board of your big picture goals for your life. If you accomplish your business goals, what are the 10 things you want out of life? Create a visual representation of your list. Use cutouts from magazines or clip art pictures—whatever it takes to develop a visual symbol of your personal goals. Post this collage to remind yourself why you work so hard. Those 10 reasons will keep you motivated on bad days as well as good ones!

By implementing these six strategies, you will be able to evaluate the effectiveness of your marketing and keep yourself motivated to stay on top of your sales processes.

Melinda F. Emerson, known as SmallBizLady, is one of America's leading small business experts. She hosts #SmallBizChat Wednesdays on Twitter 8–9 p.m. ET for small business owners. She also publishes a resource blog at http://www.succeedasyourownboss.com. Melinda is the best-selling author of *Become Your Own Boss in 12 Months; A Month-by-Month Guide to a Business That Works*.

PART EIGHT

GET BETTER PROSPECTS

☑ **45** FIVE REASONS YOU'RE GETTING REFERRED TO LOSERS— AND HOW TO FIX IT

As a marketing speaker and marketing coach, I preach and teach and continually refine my own ability to stimulate more and better referrals in addition to helping my audiences and clients do the same.

Although I am not a **referral expert**, I am indeed a **referral enthusiast.**

After reading this chapter, YOU will see where your own referral generation process may be broken—and how to fix it.

A marketing coaching client of mine asked me a great referral question: "David, I don't seem to have any problem generating referrals. In fact, my clients and colleagues are always very generous and forthcoming with referrals. The problem is not with QUANTITY—it is with QUALITY."

She went on, "No matter how successful my referral source may be, they seem to always refer me only to losers. I hate to say that, but you know what I mean. People who can't afford what we do, folks who are not decision makers, or folks who for a variety of reasons are simply not the right fit."

Her question: "How can I get out of referral jail?"

Here are five ideas to help YOU get out of referral jail and put YOUR allies, advocates, friends, and fans in the best and most likely position to refer you to the right people for the right reasons with the right fit.

1. Ask for what you want.

Be specific.

- ✳ "Business owners" is not specific. "IT managers" is not specific. "Front-line salespeople" is not specific.

- ✺ "CEOs of 20-100 person companies in the food distribution industry in the Northeast U.S." is specific.
- ✺ "Female sales executives in the technology industry" is specific.
- ✺ "IT managers in Canadian call centers" is specific.

Some of my clients also like to include a "phrase book" in their referral description. This is a collection of the phrases to listen for that indicate someone may be a good fit as a referral to you.

For a specific example of phrase book items, see my real live example online at http://www.doitmarketing.com/marketing-coach.

> The WORST kind of referral request is, "I'll talk to anybody who needs [your product/service.]"
> Stop making dumb referral requests, and you'll stop getting dumb referrals.

2. Show them names, companies, and proof that you can make those people happy.

Let's face it: the reason people don't want to give you referrals is because they're putting their own relational capital (aka reputation) on the line. And that's risky.

If you can remove the risk of the referral, you will open the floodgates to getting more and better referrals for life.

Hint: They won't believe YOU. They will believe your clients, past referrals, and people who have given you money and who have been thrilled to do so.

Print up a sheet called "Referral Success Stories." Put in five to seven specific referrals you've gotten over the last 12 months. Put in TWO kinds of quotes from both:

1. Clients who were referred and eventually hired you (client success)

2. Your referral sources who are quoting how good they looked for making the referral (referral success)

3. Tell them exactly what to say or send.

You are about to discover the power of referral blurbs. Follow the templates in the next chapter to create your own **referral blurb** and START USING IT.

4. When a bad referral comes in, give some referral coaching.

When you get referred to duds, diplomatically tell your referral sources why it wasn't a great fit AND how they can tune their radar better next time.

Here's the template you can adapt to your own situation, style, and tone. This is a delicate communication, so you will want to re-word this carefully. This is definitely not a cut-and-paste, cookie cutter response, but here's your starting point:

> Michelle,
>
> I've kindly and gently turned down the opportunity to pursue a business relationship with [referral name].
>
> Too many red flags and especially after listening to his concerns, he's just not a good fit for us.
>
> Thank you very much indeed for the referral—and, in my book, it still counts. (EVERY referral counts no matter how it turns out!)
>
> If this causes you any strain in your relationship with [referral name] (and I doubt it will), please accept my apologies in advance.
>
> For the record, his profile was perfect—**[DESCRIBE two or three ideal qualities about the referral]**. The disconnect was in our fit with his expectations and **[lack of budget, lack of need, lack of authority, whatever was missing]**—two factors over which you had no control.
>
> Always appreciate your advocacy, guidance, and friendship.
> —David

5. Ask smart Referral-giving questions to generate smart Referral-getting answers.

The fastest way to increase both the quality and quantity of your INCOMING referrals is to increase your own track record of GIVING high-quality referrals.

And to do so, you need to **stop guessing** and **start targeting.**

HOW TO BECOME A REFERRAL DETECTIVE

Learn to ask consultative questions of your current clients, vendors, partners, suppliers, friends, colleagues, and networking associates—anyone to whom you wish to GIVE more targeted referrals.

Your questions might include:

1. Who is your best client and why?
2. How did they come to you?
3. What situation were they in?
4. What did they say or do to show interest?
5. How could you tell they were a great fit?
6. How have you tried to get more just like them?
7. What should I be listening for? (Ask for details and specifics.)
8. What's the DNA of a great prospect for you? (Ask for details and specifics.)
9. What phrases, key words, or problems should I be listening for on your behalf?
10. What wants, needs, desires, and aspirations do your best clients have in common? (Ask for details and specifics.)
11. What heartaches, headaches, obstacles, and challenges do your best clients have in common? (Ask for details and specifics.)
12. If I programmed my GPS to home in on perfect prospects for you, what would those settings look like? (Ask for details and specifics.)

Be relentless in your follow-up questions to tease out details. Here's a set of probing tools to get you armed and ready for intelligent follow-up:

1. Tell me more about ...
2. Say more about ...
3. Why was that important to them?
4. What makes you say that?
5. How could you tell?
6. And that led to ...
7. Why was that a problem?
8. What else did they say?
9. What else do you think they're after?
10. Please share two or three of your favorite pre-qualification questions so that I can start to refer you more accurately

Follow these steps and you will generate MORE and BETTER referrals that are more likely to close FASTER and MORE EASILY.

46 BUILD YOUR REFERRAL BLURB

What does your **referral blurb** look like?

What? You don't know what a **referral blurb** is?
Hmmm. Don't tell me, let me guess:

* YOU are not getting enough referrals
* You'd like to get MORE referrals, but you're not sure how
* You HATE asking for referrals
* You do GREAT work. People should just refer you on the basis of your great work alone, shouldn't they?

Well, maybe all of that is true. But, as it turns out, you are living in what we marketing coaches call Referral Fantasy Land.

Want more referrals? OK, listen up.

YOU need a referral blurb. My friend, management training expert Eric David, shared this idea with me. I wanted to introduce him to the CEO of a small 10-person professional services firm, one of my clients. He said, "David, that would be great. I'll send you the e-mail."

I asked Eric, "What??"

He said, "I have an e-mail ready to go that contains everything you need to send your CEO contact about meeting me, what I do, and why it might make sense for him."

Dang! I was impressed. He went on, "I'm building my business 100 percent through three strategies: one, personal networking; two, referring good people I know to others whom they should be connected to; and three, arming my network with this paragraph of e-mail copy" (what I call his **referral blurb.**)

You want to see what this looks like, don't you? Sure you do. OK you win:

> *Dear XXX,*
>
> *I want to introduce you to my friend and colleague, Eric David. Eric is a trusted advisor in the area of management and leadership training. After meeting with Eric and hearing about his program, I think his materials and training methodology make a lot of sense (and could really benefit your organization). I suggested that you would be a great person for him to meet and feel completely comfortable asking whether you would be open to meeting him for 30 minutes or so. Based on what I know about Eric, these 30 minutes will be well worth your time, and there is no obligation if you are not interested after the half-hour meeting.*
>
> *Thanks in advance for giving this your thoughtful consideration. I'm looking forward to hearing back from you soon.*

Now, as a marketing speaker and marketing coach, I asked Eric two things:

1. Do you mind if I steal this?
2. Do you mind if I try to improve it?

He gave his blessing. So here's my version. Notice that I changed not only the business (I'm a marketing expert; he's a corporate management trainer), but I also tweaked some of the ME language into YOU language aimed at the recipient. I tried to make it more about THEM. This is key. Take a look:

> *Dear XXX,*
>
> *I want to introduce you to my friend and colleague, David Newman. David works with executives and independent professionals who want to do a better job of marketing themselves and grow their business. After meeting with David and exploring how you are currently attracting, engaging, and winning clients, you may discover that his marketing programs make sense for you (and could really benefit your bottom line). I suggested that you would be a great person for him to meet and feel completely comfortable asking whether you would be open to meeting him for 30 minutes or so.*
>
> *Based on what I know about David and his track record of helping entrepreneurs and executives succeed—even in this economy—your 30 minutes will be well spent, even if it's just to explore other ways you might be helpful to each other. Thanks in advance for giving this your thoughtful consideration.*
> *I'm looking forward to hearing back from you soon.*

OK, now it's your turn. Use this template:

> *Dear XXX,*
>
> *I want to introduce you to my friend and colleague [your name]. [first name] works with [target buyer persona] who want to [specific benefit or outcome]. After meeting with [first name] and exploring how you are currently [verb statement of an important goal of theirs], you may discover that his [topic expertise] [programs/ products/ services] make sense for you (and could*

really benefit your bottom line). I suggested that you would be a great person for him to meet and feel completely comfortable asking if you would be open to meeting him for 30 minutes or so.

Based on what I know about [first name] and his track record of helping [buyer persona category] succeed—even in this economy—your 30 minutes will be well spent, even if it's just to explore other ways you might be helpful to each other. Thanks in advance for giving this your thoughtful consideration.

I'm looking forward to hearing back from you soon.

Send your referral blurb to 10 of your trusted allies, referral partners, and close business friends. Then see how much money you'll make with this one incredibly powerful idea—**your referral blurb**!

47 DON'T BE A REFERRAL JACKASS

Wow. That's all I can say.

Sometimes a piece of marketing stupidity comes across my radar that is:

- ☀ Almost impossible to believe
- ☀ Too dumb not to share with you as a cautionary tale

Here's an e-mail I received from an audio producer whom I personally know (and who shall remain nameless to protect the moronic):

> From: Moron@AudioCoNameChanged.com
> To: David Newman <david@doitmarketing.com>
> Sent: Wednesday, February 22 3:26 PM
>
> Hi there:
> The attached is something new for 2013 which should make it easier to understand all the kinds of services we provide here at [Audio Company Name]. Hope this makes it easier to recommend us to others in the future. Thanks and hope all is well with you!

Let's review what's wrong with this picture:

1. He sends a mass e-mail to his database with the salutation, "Hi there," even though this is a guy who knows me personally, has done business with several of my clients (not on my recommendation, you can be sure), and—if he had a clue as to how to work his e-mail system—could at least have bothered to do the mass personalization required to make this note say, "Hi <fname>" to call all his contacts by name.

2. I was not really having a hard time understanding "all the kinds of services we provide here at" his company. What I do have a real hard time understanding is why anyone would refer such a self-centered goofball to their clients and prospects.

3. "Hope this makes it easier to recommend us to others in the future." Again, I was not losing a lot of sleep over how challenging it was to recommend this guy. Solving THAT problem is a priority for HIM, not for ME (or YOU for that matter). You know what would make it a lot easier for me to recommend this guy? If he actually provided me with some REAL VALUE—some insights, tips, recommendations, resources, tools, and ideas to make ME more successful, not him.

4. "Thanks and hope all is well with you!" This totally inauthentic closing simply rubs salt into an already raw wound. Is this guy

kidding? His whole tone, approach, and message are like an opera singer warming up: "ME-ME-ME-ME." And he hopes I'm doing OK while fighting throat cancer, desperately scrambling to put my parents in a nursing home, and heroically trying to make ends meet in my struggling Jewish delicatessen in the middle of the Bronx. I'm overcome with this idiot's genuine concern for me and my well-being.

The worst part of all this? He's a phony. A fake. A fraud. And a taker. This is the worst kind of small business owner there is. A snake in sheep's clothing. (Do snakes wear sheep's clothing? I dunno. This one sure does!)

You know what would have been a thousand times better?
Give me some value. Give me some REASON to want to help you. Personalize your note. Or (God forbid!) don't send me a mass e-mail at all and reach out one-on-one.

This guy has a paltry list, so it's not like one-on-one outreach to his potential advocates, allies, friends, and referral sources would be so hard to do. FYI, I don't fall into any of these categories for him (clearly!)

You want to do better than this poor sap? Sure you do. So leverage your referral blurb. Create one, share it, use it in good health.

Take the high road to referral success.

48 WORK YOUR NETWORK

If you're networking with strangers, you're wasting your time.

A consultant friend of mine once complained, "I'm doing two or three networking events a week, and I'm worn out."

When I asked why she felt networking was important, she replied, "One of my marketing goals is to do at least one networking event a week." I pointed out that she just admitted to doing two or three a week and that perhaps doing one a week is smart and doing triple that goal is causing some of the fatigue.

But there's much more to the great American business myth of networking.

Myth 1: The more you network, the more effective your networking activities become.

Truth 1: It's much more important to become well known in one or two circles than to spread your networking activities over many groups. Depth beats breadth every time.

I then asked her how networking was working for her. She replied, "I don't think I have gotten a shred of business out of it in the last six months."

Her rationale for doing networking: "Everybody knows that you build a business by networking!"

Does this make any sense? Or, worse, does it sound familiar?

See if this networking scenario has happened to you:

You meet someone at a networking breakfast. He introduces himself and mumbles something about selling real estate as you are tuning him out. He asks you what you do, and you say "IT consulting." After 10 seconds of staring blankly at each other, you both head over to refill on coffee and prune Danish for lack of anything better to do.

There has to be a better way, right? You bet. Read on.

Myth 2: The miniature wiener circuit is your path to networking success.

Truth 2: Networking with strangers to build business is about as effective as going to a singles bar to get married. In the immortal words of Dr. Phil, "It simply ain't gonna happen."

Here's why you're not going to meet your business soul mate at a networking event:

1. You aren't going to do business with people after meeting them for a few minutes and getting handed a poorly printed card.
2. Businesses are built on relationships, not on 30-second commercials, no matter how effective and intriguing.
3. Most of us have major trouble in explaining what we do, much

less getting past that explanation and listening for what prospects need.

4. Networking with strangers is not targeted or specific and, in fact, is completely random.

5. For some people, networking is exactly as effective as cold calling, which is the least effective marketing tool there is.

So am I saying that networking is a waste of time? Absolutely not. What I'm saying is that you need to start **networking smarter.** Here are a few ideas to jumpstart your networking strategy:

※ Network by having coffee or lunch with people one on one. Get to know them and their business. They may become a prospect, an alliance partner, or a referral source. But aim first and foremost to make them a friend. The rest will follow naturally.

※ If you're going to network with strangers, go with the goal of making two or three lunch or coffee dates with people you find interesting.

※ Ask every happy customer you have (they're all happy, right?) for just one referral of someone who would be interested in your type of goods or services, then call and use their name. ("Hi I'm Fred. Ginger said I should call you. Isn't Ginger great?") You already have one thing in common—Ginger!

※ Create a network hit list of the exact kind of businesses you want to network with. Maybe you sell software, and you want to meet IT managers at medium-sized companies. Make the list and put it in your little black book or smart phone. Focus your networking and outreach activities on only those people—or on others who can refer you to those people.

※ Join non-business groups and spend time doing non-business activities: civic, social, religious, recreational, musical, athletic—the list is endless. Establish relationships with people in your group. Are you into hand-drumming? Guess what? A hand-drummer will want to do business with another hand-drummer!

※ If you do go to a mixer, go with a targeted goal in mind. For example, your goal might be "to meet three people on my target list and get their cards so I can follow up for breakfast, lunch, or coffee." A traditional networking event now becomes simply the first phase of your targeted plan for global domination, not an end in itself.

Here's a final thought to shake up your networking mindset:

Network with people who already know you, like you, or have done business with you.

Myth 3: Networking is all about getting more people to know what you do.

Truth 3: Networking is all about getting people who already know you to share opportunities where you can be helpful to each other.

Make two or three phone calls a day to connect with people from past jobs, former clients, or influential people who have expressed interest in you in the past. We all have a fan base that we grossly underutilize. Think about tapping into friends, colleagues, mentors, and family to mine the connections you already have at your fingertips.

DO get out there and network, but make it worth your investment of time and energy by networking smart.

As your mother always warned you, "Don't network with strangers."

DO IT! SUCCESS STRATEGY: THE LOWEST COST, HIGHEST RETURN MARKETING STRATEGY EVER

Mark LeBlanc

Over 50 percent of my referrals come from my advocate strategy. Whether you have been in business for a long time or just recently started, here is a low-cost marketing strategy that can pay big dividends.

The Objective

The objective of this strategy is to create an advocate group. Another way to look at it is to assemble a set of fans or disciples in the marketplace.

They can be ecstatic clients, colleagues, vendors, friends, even friendly competitors. The definition of an advocate is someone who is willing to go out of his or her way to open a door or to make a positive connection on your behalf.

Put together a list of the 25 or 17 or even five most important people in your life who are in a position to impact your business. Add a few more who could be advocates if they knew you a little better!

The Next Step

Once you have your list, never let these advocates get more than 30 days away from you. That's right. You can communicate or connect with this group in one of six ways:

1. Personal visit

2. Telephone

3. Mail

4. E-mail

5. Social media

6. Text

Every 30 days, connect with your advocates in some simple way. Create an annual plan with 12 ideas for staying in touch with this special group. If these people are your advocates, it is your responsibility to stay connected with them. Although I recommend connecting with your advocates every 30 days, for some business owners, every 60 days or 90 days will work too.

Warning! As a general rule, I do not recommend that you ask your advocates for referrals. Good things will happen naturally over time. As you connect, your advocates come to know you and understand more clearly what you do and whom you do it for best.

Good Connections

Following are some simple ideas that you can include in your annual plan for staying connected with your target 25.

1. A letter

2. A book

3. A funny card

4. A button

5. A bookmark

6. A text message

7. A newsletter (quarterly means four connections for the year)

8. A holiday card

9. A phone call

10. A copy of an article you wrote

11. A coffee, lunch, or happy hour (one on one)

12. An e-mail greeting

Keep in Mind

Some people make this strategy too complicated. It should be simple. It will require from one to four hours every month. From a financial perspective, your investment can run from zero to $50 per month. Here's your chance to be creative and have some fun with people who care about your success.

Every 90 to 180 days, evaluate your list, add new advocates, and prune the people you thought were advocates. Connect with those people less regularly.

It is easy to get caught up in the trap of looking for that fancy, cutting-edge marketing strategy or magic bullet. These strategies usually look good, cost a lot, and take too much time and energy to make happen.

Your business depends on building good relationships, and referrals are a critical outcome of the marketing process. Don't let them happen by chance. You can generate more referrals with 25 advocates with whom you communicate in meaningful, personal ways every 30 days. Try it and see whether you agree with me that it is one of the most powerful marketing strategies in the world!

Mark LeBlanc started Small Business Success in 1992 and has been working with and speaking for groups of business owners and professionals who want to grow and sell more products and services.

No one has created a more comprehensive business development philosophy than Mark. His strategies are street smart and practical, and they can be easily understood and accessed. His content is driven by 16 core principles and formulas, of which any one can have immediate impact. When principles and formulas are integrated, an owner can create a wave of momentum that is unstoppable. Contact Mark at 1-800-690-0810 or Mark@SmallBusinessSuccess.com.

49 WHY YOUR INBOUND LEADS ARE A 911 CALL

When people dial 911, they need an emergency response. The sooner, the better. You get there quick, or the patient dies.

I encourage you to **UP the urgency of your marketing and sales response times.**

Why?

Well, do you know the lead follow-up time that **maximizes your sales** for online leads that come through your website or e-mail? Or your leads and prospect inquiries that come in by phone?

Do you think it's:

- a. 48 hours
- b. 24 hours
- c. 8 hours

d. 1 hour

e. 15 minutes

f. Whenever we get around to it. They can wait

Research from MarketingProfs and Hubspot proves that the lead follow-up time that maximizes sales is **within 15 minutes!**

What does that mean for you, your marketing efforts, your sales team, and your own personal schedule as a business owner or entrepreneur?

Simple: When it comes to responding to leads, the mantra is, **"Now or never."**

Bad news: Your leads won't wait; they're SEEKING a solution NOW. You are not the only service provider they are calling. Not by a long shot.

Good news: A **lead** converted to a **prospect** FAST (meaning you had a conversation within 15 minutes of first contact) are much more likely to stop looking. Once they connect with a real live human being who conveys the fact that they understand the situation AND that they are in a position to help, the frenzied dialing and e-mailing stops. All the previous unanswered calls, e-mails, and web forms go by the wayside, and YOU have YOUR shot.

So don't blow it. Don't be tempted to start waxing poetic about how great your product, your service, your program, and your people are. STOP.

A conversation that consists mostly of listening on your end is much more likely to build trust and rapport on their end.

But the point is speed. Why? Because responsiveness in the sales process signals responsiveness in the business relationship.

Quick example: I got a phone message from a prospect. I was in the car when I heard the voice mail, so I pulled over right then and there and called her back. I said, "Hi Susan, this is David Newman from Do It! Marketing." Before I could say another word, she started laughing. She said, "Well, if THIS is the kind of responsiveness I can expect when I become a client, sign me up!" And sign up she did. And she's still an active client as of this writing.

Speed is its own message.

The bottom line is that your leads CANNOT WAIT.

Because your prospects WILL NOT WAIT.

Think of your own buying behavior. You leave a message, and you keep on dialing. Someone answers, and your problem is 80 percent solved, and THAT salesperson gets the chance to win your business.

The only exception to the 911 rule is a **publicity lead**. When a reporter calls, **it's NOT a 911.**

It's a FIVE ALARM FIRE in your pants.

So if 911 is emergency response, **putting the fire out in your pants** is a critical right-now, drop-what-you're doing-this-second response. Reporters' deadlines are expressed in hours, sometimes minutes. They have hundreds of sources coming at them all day, every day. When reporters want to feature or include you in their story—RUN, don't walk to the nearest phone or Internet connection and get them what they need.

Otherwise, you're toast. And you looked so good in those pants. A real shame.

Remember: Whether it's prospects calling you to do business or journalists calling you for a story, **speed KILLS (the competition!).**

50 SEVEN STUPID WAYS TO BLOW UP YOUR SALES PROCESS

Out of frustration at my own stupidity, I posted on my blog (**www.doitmarketing.com/blog**) about the WORST sales call of my life. I ranted and raved and beat myself up for ignoring all the red flags.

Yes, it was that bad.

Let's count the ways so that YOU can apply these seven lessons to YOUR sales process. And so you never have to blow it like I did.

1. **Wrong Prospect:** I knew it in my bones even before we got on the phone. He doesn't fit, and he's missing a lot of the **DNA markers** of our most successful clients. He's sort of "out there."

2. **Wrong Process:** Did he read the material I sent ahead of time? No. Did he know what business we are in? No. Did he understand how we work and what we do—and WHY? No. Is this my prospect's fault? HELL NO! It's my fault for not following my own process (and not making sure the prospect followed it too). The only thing worse than the wrong process is NO PROCESS. And, as a marketing coach, I know I've been guilty of that in the past as well, but this time it was all on me: **I had a process that my prospect did not follow.** I should have rescheduled the moment I found this out. But I didn't.

3. **Wrong Budget:** Why, why, WHY do you keep having sales conversations with people whose initial inquiries start with the phrase "money is tight" or "our budget's been cut" or "I don't have two nickels to rub together." (I've gotten all three of these—verbatim—dozens of times, and usually I know what to do.) If they claim poverty on the approach, they will not suddenly become millionaires on the call. **Bring up money fast and early**. Not your fees, but their own pricing, their ROI, their average sale, their customer lifetime value. Do that, and you'll set the **context** for your fees as an investment. You'll be able to **avoid the sticker shock** when you drop a number on someone before you've established commensurate VALUE for them.

4. **Wrong Words:** Do you listen (TRULY listen) to what your prospects say in the first few minutes of your sales conversations? Can you identify when they are using the right words versus the wrong words to indicate their readiness to move ahead, their understanding of the value that your products and services bring, and their level of sophistication as an educated consumer? If you could, **you'd make more sales faster**, and you'd stop wasting precious selling time with price shoppers, tire kickers, and broke-ass losers.

5. **Wrong Questions:** Do you listen just as carefully—maybe more so—to the kinds of question your prospect asks YOU during the

sales call? Can you tell from THEIR questions whether they are tracking with your best clients and customers? Can you identify their underlying urgencies and priorities based on their questions? Have you ever **gently redirected a bad question** with the phrase, "The real question I'm hearing you ask is ..." "And the answer to that question is ..."? Examples of bad questions are fear-based questions that fixate on guarantees, warrantees, all that could go wrong, insignificant details, and irrelevant metrics.

6. **Wrong Bravado:** When a prospect spends any significant amount of time telling me how successful they are, how financially lucrative their business is, how much money they make, and what kind of car they drive, I know we're not a fit. Here's the truth, folks: **Successful people ARE successful. They don't TALK about being successful.** Someone who brags like this suffers from low self-esteem—or even worse, he is a mental child who is still psychologically trying to impress his mommy and daddy who never loved him enough in the first place. Move on—and quickly!

7. **Wrong Fit:** Put your current prospect in an imaginary lineup with your very favorite clients and very best customers, both past and present. Does this current prospect fit in? Do they belong there? Are they a natural extension of your business family? If not, that should be enough to get you to hang up the phone right then and there. **Like attracts like.** If your prospect would stick out like a sore thumb in your lineup of current clients, something is seriously wrong, and you should *not* allow that prospect into the circle of the clients whom you love working with—and who love working with you.

Fail to heed these seven warning signs, and the best-case scenario is that you'll waste a lot of precious time, energy, and effort on the wrong prospects who won't do business with you anyway. And the worst-case scenario is that you'll end up with a goofball client or even the nightmare client from hell.

Friends don't let friends blow up their sales process.

You're welcome.

I love you.

✓ 51 FIVE SIGNS THAT YOUR PROSPECT IS GIVING YOU TOO MUCH BS

Your marketing and sales process should be **easy, effortless, and enjoyable**.

Period. End of sentence.

If it is not—and if you're attracting **difficult, high-maintenance, or non-enjoyable** prospects—here's another marketing concept for you:

> **If the dating doesn't go well, it won't get better once you're married.**

As the great business sage, Donald Trump, once said: *"Sometimes the best deals are the ones you don't do."* Amen, brother Trump!

Five signs that your prospect is giving you too much BS

1. Agreeing to sign on and then backing off at the last minute or the next day to ask for references, birth certificates, blood tests, or guarantees.
2. Bargaining—asking for a price reduction with no corresponding reduction in services, terms, value, or relationship. (Asking for a price concession "just because" is a classic form of prospect BS!)
3. Undervaluing your services, track record, and expertise. "I could do this myself, I just don't have time" or, "We've outsourced this to several vendors and have never been happy." (Run, my friend, run!)
4. Telling you up front, "We're notoriously difficult to work with [control freaks, perfectionists, highly demanding]—but don't take it personally." This means they've fired other service providers in

the past, and they're prepping you for the same eventuality while playing BOTH sides of good cop–bad cop. Nice!

5. Using terms of false affection, like "Big Guy" and "My dear," or false compliments, like "You're a great salesperson!" (Obviously, if you were a great salesperson, you wouldn't be wasting your time with this narcissistic sociopath nightmare client from hell, would you?)

As poet Maya Angelou has so eloquently said, **"When someone SHOWS you who they are, believe them."**

52 YOUR NINE-POINT CLIENT GPS

GPS stands for Goofball Prevention Screening, and here's why you need one.

Every day here at Do It! Marketing HQ, we work hard to make sure the clients we love are extremely happy with our work and our results.

At the same time, we work hard to keep OUT clients who will make us nuts, sap our energy, or for whom it will be impossible to do our best work.

And you should do the same in your business.

In this spirit, here is an example to model if you'd like to create your company's very own Client GPS tool (Goofball Prevention Screening).

A client may well prove to be a goofball if they:

1. **Lack high standards of excellence:** Good enough is good enough.
2. **Don't care about increasing their knowledge:** They are not

committed to becoming valuable resources to their own clients and customers.

3. **Refuse to work hard and commit to their own success:** They lack persistence and are unwilling to try new things to achieve results.

4. **Think they already know everything:** They are unwilling to accept help in expanding their skills, expertise, or capabilities.

5. **Resist investing in themselves and their business:** They fail to understand that this is the best investment of all.

6. **Operate from a mindset of fear and scarcity:** They can't make good long-term decisions because they are so risk averse in the short term.

7. **Won't (or can't) pay their bills:** Their lack of financial responsibility spills over onto others in the form of late payment, nonpayment, and endless excuses.

8. **Exude negative energy:** With a lot of negative self-talk, pessimism, and cynicism, they repel new opportunities, new partners, and new ideas (all vital to success).

9. **Can't commit to mutually supportive relationships:** In business and in life, the most successful people don't make it alone.

That's my list. Are you ready? It's YOUR turn to make yours.

My client might be a goofball if they:

1. _____
2. _____
3. _____
4. _____
5. _____
6. _____
7. _____
8. _____
9. _____

✓ 53 HOW GOOD OF A CLIENT WILL YOU BE?

The phone rings and it's my friend Steve who is a fellow speaker and consultant. He said to me at the beginning of the call, "David, I'm calling you for a reference."

So I'm thinking, "OK, he wants to hire someone I've hired or someone I know—perhaps even a client of mine whose testimonial he saw on my website."

I say, "Steve, what can I do for you?"

And then he mentions someone's name. Let's call this person Larry. Now I like Larry, and he's a good guy. Perhaps he's a little confused about his marketing and messaging, and that's OK because Larry is NOT a client of mine (although I've given him plenty of chances!).

I start to answer Steve, and he stops me: "No, no. I don't want to hire Larry. Larry wants to hire me. I'm calling you to ask you what kind of client do you think he would be?"

Wow. It's not a consultant reference, speaker reference, or service provider reference. Steve was asking me, "Would this guy be a good client?" FYI, Steve saw me connected to Larry through LinkedIn and some other social media sites.

Lessons for you:

* We live in a hyperconnected world.
* People DO read your social media profiles.
* People DO judge you on the company you keep, both online and off.
* If you're a pain in the ass—as a consultant, vendor, partner, OR client—word will spread faster than you can imagine.
* The top people in their field (ahem, YOU) do not have the bandwidth for nor the interest in working with folks who are a pain in the butt.
* YOU can't afford to be a pain in the butt on either side of the buying equation.

PART NINE

ELIMINATE
ROADBLOCKS

54 RBI MEETS CSI

Have you ever been rejected out of hand by a prospect who not only **doesn't understand** what you DO but—as a bonus—tells you that **they already have it taken care of** in-house?

It's like they're saying, "Uh, I don't know what that is, but we already have that here."

This is what I call **rejection by ignorance (RBI)**. And it is one of the most frustrating things you'll run into as a marketing or sales executive—and certainly as an entrepreneurial business owner.

Quick example from my world—see how this story plays out in the context of **YOU and YOUR products, services, and value proposition . . .**

First, a bit of background. **As a marketing speaker and marketing coach**, I market and sell to two audiences:

1. For **marketing coaching,** I market to business owners, consultants, and professional services firms who want to grow.
2. For **speaking,** I market to large companies, conferences, associations, and various industry groups made up of business owners and executives who want to market smarter.

In this chapter, **you will pick up some tools for marketing YOUR products and services better, smarter, and faster**—and you'll also see how to avoid one of the STUPIDEST sales rejections ever.

Ready? Strap in—this could get ugly.

Oh, wait! . . .

First, let me share a really good speaker prospecting letter with you.

I use this one to get back in touch with speaking clients and also to cross-sell and upsell along the geographic hierarchy (local—state—regional—national) of organizations I've already spoken for.

(All names changed to protect . . . well, you know!) Here it is:

> Dear Glenda,
>
> I'm hoping you can help me. I'm trying to get in touch with the person responsible for selecting speakers for your [organization name] national conferences for two reasons:
>
> 1. To invite them to a conversation about exploring our possible fit for your speaker roster next year. I presented an extremely well-received keynote at the regional [organization name] conference last year and would love to do more for [organization name].
>
> The conference promo from last year is attached for your reference, and the special welcome video I did for your group is here [YouTube link]:
>
> 2. If a high-energy, high-content marketing program is not a fit, I can recommend several other outstanding professional speakers to you because of my active involvement and leadership roles within the National Speakers Association.
>
> Please do get back to me, and let me know your thoughts.
> David Newman
> [signature block]

So far, so good. And please DO use this letter template if you're a speaker, consultant, or executive who uses speaking to generate leads and revenue for your firm.

(And yes, you're very welcome!)

Now here's where things get stupid.

Glenda forwarded my note to their national HQ. Then I got this brief response from HQ. Please keep your eye out for the RBI—rejection by ignorance.

> Glenda forwarded your e-mail to me. I work with our conferences and events. Because of our arrangement with [corporate HQ], we do not have marketing speakers on our programs. [Our organization] has their own marketing division and provides the marketing support to all offices in the country, so it is not part of our professional development portfolio.

As best as I can tell, she's telling me, **"Uh, we have a department that does that."**

That's funny because I've presented seminars and workshops for 44 of the Fortune 500 global corporations, and I'm pretty sure THEY all have marketing departments, too!

By this logic, no large company would hire a **sales consulting firm** because:

They have a sales department.

No large organization would hire an **outside training company** because:

They have a training department.

No multinational corporation would use a **recruiting firm** because (say it with me now):

They have a recruiting department.

So what should YOU do to avoid (or recover from) RBI?

Acknowledge it—love it—embrace it.

Corollary: If you can't market and sell to ignorant people who give you stupid excuses, you're going to have a very brief career in sales.

Oh, damn! Was this microphone on?

Back to the story.

The tricky part is that you never know when you're going to run into this particular brand of stupidity, so I don't recommend doing anything differently up front.

Once **RBI** rears its ugly head, your best chance at a recovery is what I call **CSI.** This stands for **Complement and Supplement In-house efforts.**

Here's a sample phone conversation or an e-mail reply to little Susie Creamcheese* at the global HQ of the Moron Corporation above:

> Susie,
>
>   Thank you for your note. I understand completely.
>
>   Most organizations that I work with also have a robust marketing department.
>
>   These organizations value our programs precisely because I

---

* "Little Susie Creamcheese" is a favorite saying of my speaking colleague, sales expert David Yoho. Hire him. He's awesome.

> *help them with strategies, tactics, and tools that **complement***
> ***and supplement what they're already doing in-house.***
>
> *I'm attaching a brief overview of the program I'm proposing, along with five testimonial letters from clients in your industry who have a strong central marketing function AND who had great things to say about the results of our work together.*
>
> *Worth a 10-minute phone conversation? Let me know either way and thanks in advance for considering it.*
>
> *David Newman*
> *[signature block]*

Boo-yah! Eat that, Jack.

RBI has met CSI, and it's game over.

Hope that was as good for you as it was for me.

55 BECOME THE MISSING PIECE

A number of years ago, a boutique consulting firm hired me to help them market a career management course for new and emerging leaders.

The program was a hybrid of personal and professional development for high-potential leaders inside large organizations. The program was terrific, but, when they first came to me, they were having difficulty describing it succinctly to their prospective clients. I recommended that they use the next level of CSI and BECOME the "missing piece" that prospects didn't even know they were missing!

This tactic is a combination of clear articulation with a very specific type of visual imagery. Here's how it can work for YOU!

Imagine that you are selling a specialized product, service, or program and that one of your most common marketing stumbling blocks is that people feel they are already doing something similar.

Embrace that objection, and include it in your marketing materials. Here's how we handled it for my career management client. We developed a Marketing Language Bank that included the following sections:

1. The Problem
2. The Solution
3. Is This Right for Your Organization?
4. How Does This Work?
5. What Do You Get?
6. Who Is This for?
7. Aren't We Already Doing This?
8. How Is This Program Different?
9. Benefits at a Glance
10. What Are the Outcomes of the Program?

The key to this strategy is in item 7, "Aren't We Already Doing This?" You need to address head-on the fact that NO, they are not doing this already or that. If they are, they aren't doing it consistently enough, often enough, or thoroughly enough.

Then you need to bolster your claims with highly credible third-party research, industry statistics, quotes from professional experts, or other sources that your prospects are likely to recognize and respect.

Putting it all together, here's an example of the language you can model yours from:

AREN'T WE ALREADY DOING THIS?

You may think so. However, research shows that you're probably not doing enough career development or not doing it for the right people in the right way.
Research from HR.com and the Institute for Corporate Productivity showed that **over 40 percent of organizations of all sizes do not**

have any formal career development program. *Another 24 percent leave career development tasks strictly to their in-house managers, mentors, and coaches, usually as part of the performance review process. This clearly is not enough.* Of the organizations surveyed, **over 80 percent reported plans to launch or expand their career development offerings.**

Long-term career focus is what separates your best people— who maximize your HR investment, stay, thrive, and contribute the most—from the mediocre contributors who drain your time, effort, and profitability.

This program is a perfect complement or supplement to the leadership development and executive education you may already be doing. However, these are no substitute for giving your high-potential leaders the **specific, clear, and focused career management skills that they need.**

To accompany this powerful language, the specific visual imagery I recommend is a series of four arrows with the typical products, services, and processes that most of your customers are already using in ONE color and **your product/service in the third position in a contrasting color.**

A picture is worth a thousand words, so here's what it looks like:

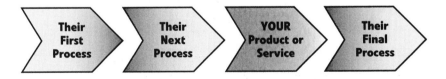

Now your marketing conversation can naturally center on how your offerings fit right in, solve a problem, close a gap, address a lack, or otherwise make for a "perfect fit!"

The beauty of this diagram is its simplicity. You don't even need to show your prospects a web page, brochure, or data sheet with this graphic. You can simply grab a pen and draw it on a napkin, notepad, or scrap of paper as you're talking with them in person.

Final note: Don't mess with the graphic. Clients have taken this idea and gotten creative (against my strong advice) by using pyramids, concentric circles, linked rectangles, and a host of other meaningless visuals. The business owners and professionals who stuck with my arrows consistently report how effective it is in closing sales (along with the accompanying prospect conversation). And the ones that screwed with the graphic still struggle to get their point across to buyers. Work with the arrows and the arrows will work for YOU!

56 STOP WASTING YOUR TIME FOLLOWING UP

Confession: I read roughly 100 marketing, sales, and business development books per year. And in almost every one, you'll hear something similar to these bits of advice about sales follow-up:

* "The fortune is in the follow-up."
* "If you don't follow up five to seven times, you'll lose the sale."
* "Nobody ever, EVER buys on the first, second, or third appointment."
* "Most sales are made after the eighth contact, but most salespeople stop after the third contact."

I have good news: This advice is **horse doo–doo,** and it's probably **making you needlessly tired, frustrated, and depressed.**

I also have bad news: This advice is **STINKY horse doo–doo** that is costing you face-to-face time with REAL decision makers.

Here are seven reasons you're wasting your time with follow-up:

1. **If you're focused exclusively on prospects who are actively SEEKING** to solve the problem you're positioned to solve, you'll get their attention on the first or second attempt. If you don't get

their attention, then you need more targeted and relevant prospects.

2. **You're marketing in an era where everyone—including (and especially) your prospects—are moving at 100 mph.** Life moves too fast for follow-up. You're either an immediate priority or invisible.

3. **Leave non-prospects the hell alone.** Continuing to "check in" for no good reason when you're in the invisible column gets real annoying real fast. You will damage your chances at future sales when you're a current pest.

4. **Decision makers make decisions.** If you're stuck in follow-up hell, you weren't dealing with a real decision maker in the first place. Following up with someone with no check-writing authority is like trying to teach a Labrador retriever to drive. It may be fun for a short time, but then someone is going to get bitten.

5. **"Short attention span theater" rules the day.** If you follow up with today's hot prospect next month, the chances are excellent that your prospect will say, "Who are you again? You talked about what? When? I'm sorry, I'm just running to a meeting. Bye!"

6. **Alpha dogs BUY—Sheep dogs BARK.** The chances are that, no matter what your product or service, if you're selling to a decision maker, that person has an alpha dog personality. They are Drivers on the DISC® Profile, and they make fast decisions with a very low threshold of patience for dickering, bureaucracy, or delay. If you want to make a fast sale, the *REAL* buyer is your best ally to make that happen. Or not. But following up to drag out the process will simply turn them off.

7. **If you relentlessly focus on the right prospects at the right time for the right reasons,** you'll spend a whole lot less time convincing and persuading fence-sitters and a whole lot more time focusing like a laser beam on the buyers who are ready, willing, and eager to do business with you. No follow-up needed.

TWO QUICK EXAMPLES

Dave—The No-Follow-Up Sales Champ

When I was working for a large enterprise software firm, I sat across from one of our top inside salespeople on the days that he and I were both in the office. Those days were a rare treat because I could overhear Dave's sales calls between my own meetings and calls. Talk about free sales training. Dave was masterful.

Dave would call hand-selected leads who were, more often than not, Fortune 1000 chief information officers (CIOs). His opening question after a seven-second introduction of his name and company went something like this:

> *I don't know if you're currently evaluating options for enterprise software, but if you are, I can offer you some insights and recommendations in less than 15 minutes to help you make a better decision, whether that's with us or not. Is ERP software on your agenda for this year?*

Yes. No. Boom. He opened conversations with about 70 percent of these prospects.

The other 30 percent politely disqualified themselves, and he never called them again.

If you're not looking to invest in this category of software BEFORE Dave called you, nothing he said by way of follow up would make you dig into the corporate budget and come up with an extra $1–2 million, which was his average sale.

Dave made a note in his CRM database to call them next year. Sometimes he would get the same CIO. Sometimes he would connect with the new CIO because the previous guy botched the ERP installation they bought from someone else. In any case, each annual call was a qualification call: a yes/no filter, NOT a follow-up.

Colleen—The SuperAchiever Coach with the No-Follow-Up Sales Letter

My pal Colleen Bracken and I started our speaking and coaching businesses within a few months of each other back in 2001. In her early days, Colleen specialized in what she called "SuperAchiever coaching"—working with CEOs, government leaders, and other top dogs in the corporate and non-profit world.

We worked together on crafting a **no-follow-up sales letter**. Why? Because Colleen had ZERO interest in chasing prospects. She wanted to make this clear in her sales process because she also knew that the alpha dogs she was selling to felt the same way.

Here is a portion of the letter we put together:

> If you know someone (perhaps someone sitting in your chair?) who is ready to embark on the short, fast, exhilarating ride to the next level of success, STRAP IN and call me at [phone number] or e-mail me at [e-mail address]. You'll set up your **no-risk no-obligation 15-minute SuperAchiever coaching call.** You'll be amazed at what we can do in a quarter of an hour.
>
> Finally, I need to answer your unasked question: **Why should you work with me?** After all, we've both been doing just fine without each other so far, right?
>
> 1. I've **handpicked** you as someone I specifically want to work with.
>
> 2. I'm a **REAL professional coach.** I've received my PCC certification, which means that I've studied 250 hours, coached for 1,000 hours, and have been designated by the International Coach Federation (the world governing body of the coaching profession). **Only 275 other coaches (out of 35,000 coaches worldwide) in the world** have met this standard.
>
> 3. **Clients I've worked with have had this to say** about our professional relationship:

[Colleen inserts three of her most powerful short testimonials from other alpha dogs whom the recipient would recognize and respect.]

Invest 15 minutes with me—no-risk, no obligation—then **decide for yourself.** What's the worst that could happen? You spend 15 minutes **getting my best ideas, questions, and tools around what you're working on right now**, and we part ways.

Or throw this letter straight into recycling. Only you know whether you're ready for this personal, powerful, unique stuff and the breakthrough successes that come with it.

Colleen

[Signature block]

PS: You're working at 100 mph, and so am I. For this reason, I won't bother to follow up with you. In my experience, Super-Achievers make fast decisions. So I figure I'll be hearing from you in the **next 3–5 days. Or not at all.**

PPS: It's your move.

With this approach in her letters, e-mails, and personal networking, Colleen built her extremely successful leadership coaching, training, and speaking business.

The moral of the story? Screw follow-up.

You hate doing it. They hate receiving it.

Instead, do everything in your power to market, sell, and profit from **prospects who are eager to open the door for you when you knock!**

DO IT! SUCCESS STRATEGY: WHY PEOPLE DON'T RETURN YOUR PHONE CALLS AND HOW TO FIX IT

Barry Moltz

Here comes that sinking feeling again. The prospect you have been meeting didn't return your phone call yesterday. In fact, you have not heard from her all week. You call again, and still nothing. The silence baffles you. You worked hard to land this customer. You thought the sale was nearly closed. This one was a sure thing.

Why don't people return your phone calls?

We are not talking about cold calls. In that case, a returned call is a bonus. We are discussing return calls from people you have actually talked to many times before—calls to people you have met with, had lunch with, or maybe even done business with.

This pattern of unanswered calls can still amaze many of us. We need to realize that a few weeks of unreturned phone calls means that the answer is no to whatever you want to talk about or that the person no longer values your relationship. In fact, I yearn for them to leave a voice mail in the middle of the night when my cell phone is off and yell: "Barry, you screwed it up. Don't ever call me again, you moron." That message I understand and respect.

Why don't people just call or e-mail and be blunt? With all the electronic and increasingly impersonal ways to communicate with each other, why has this task not become easier for people?

The three reasons are:

1. People are just too busy and overbooked. Their rush to multitask, unfortunately, overruns even some basic human courtesies.

2. Technology has created too many contact points. While our expectations are high with all the possible instant communication methods, handling all of them has become increasingly difficult. The average businessperson needs to check messages by way of multiple phone, e-mail, and social media accounts.

3. People are cowards. It takes courage to confront someone and say no. Most busy people don't want to take the time to deal with it. They find it easier to ignore it.

The Rapid Release Strategy

Here is how to get your phone call returned and what to do if it does not get returned:

1. Make the initial call. Leave specific instructions on the desired action you need and a timeframe in which you would like to be called back.

2. If no answer, call back in a week.

3. If no answer, call back in two weeks.

4. In no answer, send a note or leave a voice mail with the following-message:

> Dear John,
>
> I have been unsuccessful in my attempts to reach you and pro-vide the information you requested. This typically means:
>
> 1. You've been busy but are still very interested talking with me about how I can help.
>
> 2. You are no longer interested.
>
> Being a businessperson, I know you can appreciate my posi-tion.
>
> I want to provide you with excellent customer service and all of the information you require to make an educated decision that will benefit your business. What I don't want to do is bother you with something if you are no longer interested.
>
> Could you please help me by letting me know which of the two situations we are in? This will allow me to better allocate my time while still providing you with the amount of attention you desire.

If there is still no answer, forget them as a current prospect, no matter how much work it took to get to this point. Put them back into the marketing funnel and dial another prospect.

A "no" answer, even though not optimal, is as important as a "yes" because it allows you to move on and close the door. With limited time, a "no" allows you to focus on the prospects who still can say "yes."

Why should YOU return every phone call or e-mail from people with whom YOU have a relationship? It's just good business. Our careers rise and fall with unpredictable economic times. We meet the same people on the way up as we meet on the way down. In other words, today you need something from me, and tomorrow I need something from you. If I never returned your phone call when you needed me, what do you think will happen when the roles are reversed? Communicating in a respectful way will build the critical relationship capital with other people that you need for your business success.

Have you returned all your calls today?

Barry Moltz is a nationally recognized expert on entrepreneurship who has given hundreds of presentations to audiences ranging in size from 20 to 20,000.

Barry is the acclaimed author of four chart-topping business books. His first book, *You Need to Be a Little Crazy: The Truth About Starting and Growing Your Business*, describes the ups and downs and emotional trials of running a business. It is in its fifth reprint and has been translated into four languages. His second book, *Bounce! Failure, Resiliency and the Confidence to Achieve Your Next Great Success*, shows what it takes to come back and develop true business confidence. His third book, *BAM! Delivering Customer Service in a Self-Service World*, shows how customer service is the new marketing. And his fourth book, *Small Town Rules*, shows how in a connected economy—where every customer can talk to every other customer—it's like living in a small town.

Connect with Barry at www.barrymoltz.com.

Prospects who BUY from you should get a fabulous
seven-course feast.

But even prospects who DON'T buy from you should get a Happy Meal®.

That's right: Nobody leaves hungry.

Here's what I mean.

Look at your marketing materials. The key question is, "Will people keep your marketing materials even if they don't do business with you?"

Are you providing REAL value?

Is your message more about THEM and THEIR problems and their solutions than about YOU and YOUR SERVICES and YOUR CREDENTIALS?

The bottom line is that nobody cares about YOU. Period. All they care about is what ideas you have for them, how you can help them reach THEIR goals, and how your solution makes their life easier, better, or more profitable.

Of all the things you send out—your sales letters, brochures, newsletters, e-zines, presentation kits—everything should be a KEEPER.

Question: How can you make sure the stuff you send out CAN'T be thrown away?

Answer: Make it valuable, relevant, educational, shareable, and referenceable.

Here's an example from an industry that you might think is completely commoditized: digital printing. (For digital printing companies who don't heed this advice, they ARE!)

Over 10 years ago, I met a sales guy, Gary, from a company called Digital Color Graphics in the Philadelphia area, where I live. We had a great conversation, and exchanged business cards. He then asked me whether it was OK if he sent me something in the mail. I said, "Sure" and left the meeting, not giving it another thought.

The next day, I got an eight-page glossy well-designed newsletter from Digital Color Graphics. At first, I'm reading it over the recycling bin, thinking this was just another glossy brochure telling me what a great print shop they are.

I could not have been more wrong.

First of all, there was a very well put together sidebar on the front cover with a table of contents. There were 8–10 different articles, tips, checklists, and ideas in this brochure—for me and my business. Nothing necessarily about printing, but about small business marketing, sales, business development, client attraction, negotiating tips, PR ideas, and resource lists of cool online and offline tools to grow your business.

Now don't get me wrong: I WANTED to throw this thing away.

I really did. My office is already piled high with magazines, books, articles, folders. I'm endlessly fighting the Battle of the Piles, so one more brochure was NOT something I wanted to keep.

But I had to keep it. It was too damn good to throw away.

- ✺ It was **referenceable**: I wanted to keep it for future reference and research some of the recommended resources in more depth.
- ✺ It was **shareable**: I could look smart by sharing some of these resources with my own circle of clients, prospects, friends, and collaborators.
- ✺ It was **educational**: It contained original and clever tips, suggestions, and ideas that I had not seen elsewhere.

Did they pitch any printing? Not really.

A quarter of the back page talked about their services and how they'd be happy to discuss any of the marketing and promotional ideas in the newsletter if you wanted to explore how to apply them in your business.

Question: What are YOU sending out that's too good for your prospects to throw away?

Think tip sheets, checklists, resources, action steps, samples, booklets, articles, how-to guides, etc.

The more value you provide in your marketing, the more you are reinforcing the idea, "Wow! This person is sharing this great information with EVERYBODY. Imagine what we'd get if we became CLIENTS!"

On the flip side of this equation, I also recommend that you continue to deliver tons of great value to your clients—**even after they've stopped paying you.**

That's right: Become known as someone who delivers great value BEFORE the sale, DURING the relationship, and long AFTER your clients stop paying you. Your job is to create a 24/7 FEAST for prospects, customers, and past customers too!

Here's a testimonial I use all the time to reinforce the feast idea:

> "David Newman has to be the hardest working guy in sales and marketing. Even after we finished working together, I would get e-mails from David about another idea he had for us. He far surpasses any course I have ever taken, any tapes or books I have read. You cannot hire a better person for your company than David Newman."
>
> Mary Broussard, CEO, The Barter Connection

What are you doing to generate testimonials like this one?

Keep your clients well fed with valuable ideas before, during, AND after the sale, and you'll be well on your way!

PART TEN

YOUR BUSINESS DNA

58 BRANDING IS BS

"Branding is everything—and I mean everything."
—SCOTT BEDBURY

"Branding is overrated."
—REGIS MCKENNA

I'm going with Regis McKenna on this one.

There is so much hot air being blown around about brands and branding, by everyone from the brilliant (Tom Peters and "Brand You!") to the absurd (hundreds of so-called branding coaches who have glommed onto branding as a buzzword and refuse to let go).

"Small business branding" is often code for a lot of BS from marketing consultants and ad agencies who are more interested in what's in your wallet than in what will grow your business and make your phone ring.

I'm going to define **brand** very clearly and plainly.

A brand is a promise of an experience. Period.

You walk into a McDonald's for lunch versus a Ritz-Carlton Hotel because that's the kind of lunch you want that day. You would probably be confused and more than a little upset if you found waiters and linen tablecloths in that McDonald's or if your lunch bill came to $110.

So, to punch through a lot of the mystique around building a brand—especially for business owners and entrepreneurs like you—let's call it a promise.

* Who can make a promise? Anyone.
* How much does it cost to make a promise? Usually nothing.
* Can you make a promise to someone across the hall? Sure.
* Across the country? You bet.
* Can you make promises to people in just your local area? Of course.

- ✹ Do you need to be crystal clear on what that promise means before you try to communicate it to others? Yes, that would be smart.
- ✹ If asked, could your top executives say what your promise is or means? Would the answers be consistent?
- ✹ Hmmm . . .

"Brand" means a few simple things:

- ✹ Brand is communication.
- ✹ Brand is consistency.
- ✹ Brand is integrity.
- ✹ Brand is the ongoing recognition for a job consistently well done.

Boiling all these timeless business ideas into a five-letter word doesn't change them.

✓ 59 YOUR NAME SUPPORTS EVERYTHING YOU DO

Many years ago, a client of mine launched a new professional services business venture. She identified **responsible leadership** as her expertise and distinction in the marketplace. She wanted to name her company Responsible Leadership, Inc. and build it out under the domain she had already bought, www.ResponsibleLeadership.com.*

---

* *Note:* Against my advice but for good reasons of her own, my client decided to go in a different direction with her company name, and the domain currently belongs to a leadership program at the Queen's University School of Business in Ontario, Canada.

She asked me what I thought of that name. I told her, **"We gotta be careful."**

The name is **not** going to just stand on its own. It's going to become your methodology, your approach, your brand, and the **through line that connects all of your offerings.**

Soooo, make sure you love all of the following too. (Go ahead and **plug in YOUR brand or YOUR words** that articulate your fabulousness):

- Responsible Leadership Assessment
- Responsible Leadership Retreats
- Responsible Leadership Survey
- Responsible Leadership Seminar
- Responsible Leadership Training
- Responsible Leadership Coaching
- Responsible Leadership IQ
- Responsible Leadership Conference
- Responsible Leadership News
- Responsible Leadership Blog
- Responsible Leadership E-zine
- Responsible Leadership Summit
- Responsible Leadership Tools
- Responsible Leadership Certification
- Responsible Leadership—the book
- Responsible Leadership—the keynote
- Responsible Leadership—the MBA guest lecture
- Responsible Leadership—the podcast
- Responsible Leadership—the PBS special
- Responsible Leadership—the video series
- Responsible Leadership—the e-learning course
- Responsible Leadership—the six-month leadership development course
- . . . and so on!

So naming your company is no joke. And I'm not just saying that because I'm a marketing speaker and marketing coach and do this work all day long for a living! It really is a BIG, far-reaching decision.

You want everything to line up under your brand so that you get a self-reinforcing marketing system where all the pieces fit and click—or, in sales speak, so that you have plenty of opportunities for cross-selling, up-selling, and cross-pollination.

You want to own the thought leadership platform around your name and your offerings.

Question: How does YOUR company-naming empire stack up?

60 BMW AT ONE DOLLAR OVER INVOICE!

In a scene from *The Simpsons*, Homer gets to play softball with major league baseball stars who have been recruited to play on his company team. He's sitting in the locker room with New York Yankees great Darryl Strawberry, and Homer asks him, "Hey, do you play baseball better than me?"

Strawberry pauses for a moment, looks at Homer, and replies, "I don't know you . . . but yes."

Likewise, I don't know you . . . but your prices are too low.

And you're probably also charging for your time and not for your VALUE. That's another major league mistake.

But let's take a moment to discuss high prices. **Think of any product or service that is known for its high price**—Chanel No. 5 perfume, a BMW, or a $25,000 Rolex.

What are some associations you make with the high-priced provider of a product or service? If you're like most folks in my seminars and workshops, your answers include:

- ✳ They must be . . . **Proven**
- ✳ They must be . . . **Smart**
- ✳ They must be . . . **Well made**
- ✳ They must be . . . **Worth it**
- ✳ They must be . . . **Prestigious**
- ✳ They must be . . . **Respected**
- ✳ They must be . . . **Exclusive**

Now what are some associations you make with low-priced providers of those same products or services?

- ✳ They must be . . . **Fly-by-night**
- ✳ They must be . . . **Be low-average**
- ✳ They must be . . . **Flimsy**
- ✳ They must be . . . **Unreliable**
- ✳ They must be . . . **Not valuable**
- ✳ They must be . . . **Risky**

Final thought: Have you ever seen a BMW dealer advertise in those screaming commercials, "Come on down! We have cars one dollar over invoice!" Of course not. That's not who they are, and that's not how they want to be perceived.

And same goes for you. Class it up. You'll get better clients, more profitable customers, less price resistance, and more sales.

Don't be afraid of creating REAL value, and don't be shy about getting **well paid** for it.

✓ **61** YOU'RE COMPETING WITH IDIOTS—AND THEY'RE WINNING

Here's the problem for you:

- ✸ You have integrity
- ✸ You have smarts
- ✸ You have standards
- ✸ You have ethics
- ✸ You have conscientiousness
- ✸ You have detail orientation
- ✸ You have an innate desire to deliver only your best work
- ✸ Why is any of this a problem

Because you're competing with idiots who:

- ✸ Charge more (way more in some cases)
- ✸ Deliver less (way less in MOST cases)
- ✸ Shoot faster
- ✸ Shoot more often
- ✸ Brag and boast with nothing but hot air and smoke
- ✸ Overpromise and package their offerings with more sizzle
- ✸ Underdeliver but become brilliant at evasion and deceit
- ✸ Game the system to win meaningless awards, garner inflated reviews, and continue to deceive the world that they are better than you

Truth: They're not better than you at all. Not for a second.

But here's the rub: Perception is reality. **Let me repeat that: Perception IS reality.**

- ✸ You're fighting the wrong war
- ✸ You're trying to win the wrong game

- You are who Google says you are
- Your clients see what your LinkedIn recommendations tell them to look for

You are really fighting a two-front war:

1. Managing the **perceptions** of you and your company
2. Managing the **reality** of you and your company

> The fakers are better at **faking it**. So you better be better at **delivering it**. For real. For every minute of every day.

If perception is reality, then the sooner you get busy changing the perception of you, the sooner your prospects and clients will appreciate your reality.

Keep it real, people.

DO IT! SUCCESS STRATEGY: HOW CRM SYSTEMS CAN CUT YOUR EXPENSES AND SAVE YOUR BACON

Gene Marks

As a CPA, I've learned a lot about reducing costs over the past 15 years. Sometimes from an unlikely place too. Like customer relationship management (CRM) systems. This technology can help you reduce costs. Really.

How is this done? Here are a few things I've learned.

By creating workflows, you can save time.

My roofer, a longtime CRM user, taught me something about using his CRM system to save time. When a new job comes in for him, at least 20 tasks need to be performed, including ordering materials, sending thank-you notes, and scheduling trucks. He asked me to help him configure work-flows in his CRM system so that, with one click of the button, all of these tasks were accomplished, along with reminders and alerts to ensure that nothing fell through the cracks.

And it worked! So if you're spending too much time doing repetitive tasks, you might find that automating these tasks in your CRM system will cut labor hours and increase productivity too.

If you know about something before it happens, you can prepare.

Have you ever dealt with a Genius-in-His-Own-Mind customer? The one who takes up everyone's time but doesn't pay his bills? What's the secret to dealing with him? It's letting everyone know in advance who he is and nipping his antics in the bud.

I know a few smart business owners who use their CRM systems to help them deal with the dreaded Genius in His Own Mind. They set record alerts and run reports so that, if someone like him calls, everyone immediately knows what to do. These customers can be identified as early as possible and, as Tony Soprano would say, dealt with. Remember: It's business, just business.

The more your website talks, the more your database listens.

A guy I know, John, drums up new clients for his insurance business by running seminars. Mainly he gets a group of retired people looking for free dinners. In the past, people would call his office to register, and the recep-tionist would fill out forms, send confirmation materials, and then send reminder materials. Try doing that for a hundred people a month. Try feed-ing baked chicken to this same crowd. Not pretty.

But many now use the Internet. So John configured his CRM system to import this feature from his website. Now, those who want to attend one of his seminars go to his website and fill out a form; the data gets sent to his CRM system automatically. Using workflows, his system creates a record and then automatically sends registration and reminder e-mails as well as survey results and follow-up actions to his salespeople.

Not only has this cut back on administrative time, but it's improved response time too. His seminars are now cheaper to produce. His sales turnaround time is less, meaning that his salespeople can work on more people in the same amount of time. The chicken's still pretty dry, though.

Finally, looking stupid costs money.

My wife is from England and goes to England frequently to visit her family. She takes the same flight from our local airport every time—for 20 years! Do the people there recognize her? No. Offer her a free Coke? No. Greet her warmly? No. Now she looks at other airlines where she can be treated better. That airline has lost her business on many an occasion.

With a good CRM system, your business doesn't have to be this way. As long as everyone in the office is keeping things up-to-date, whenever a customer calls in, whoever picks up the phone can act like a best friend. "Why hello Mr. Kline. How are those ... Dodgers ... doing? And your son ... Max ..., is he out of jail yet? He is? Super. I see here that Maria spoke to you a few days ago about the question you had. Is there something I can help you with?"

Good CRM systems help you avoid looking like a dope in front of your customers. That saves the cost of losing a good customer or two, eh?

See? Good CRM systems don't just increase sales. I've learned that they can decrease costs and save your bacon too.

Gene Marks is a former senior manager at KPMG and, since 1994, the owner of the Marks Group PC, a highly successful 10-person CRM consulting firm based outside Philadelphia. Through his keynotes, workshops, seminars, and executive retreats, Gene helps business owners, executives, and managers understand the political, economic, and technological trends that will affect their companies so that they can make profitable decisions.

Gene has written five small-business management books, most recently, *In God We Trust, Everyone Else Pays Cash: Simple Lessons from Smart Business People*. His online columns for *Forbes*, *Huffington Post*, *BusinessWeek*, *The New York Times*, and *Philadelphia Magazine* are read by thousands of business owners each week. Connect with Gene at www.MarksGroup.net.

62 DIVERSIFY WHILE STILL SPECIALIZING

As a proactive business strategy and a wise form of marketing insurance, this idea is powerful and laden with interesting possibilities for you and your business.

Never put all your eggs in one basket; instead, have several separate baskets in your business.

Now, you still can't yield to the temptation to sell everything to everyone. Develop two parallel offerings or divisions or brands that tap into your unique expertise but that appeal to different populations, industries, needs, or audiences. (I'm NOT talking about a management consultant who also sells real estate on the side!)

Afraid that you'll carve a niche that's too narrow? Listen, there's a place in New York City that just sells rice pudding, called Rice to Riches. That's specializing.

How do they diversify? They make money when you eat at their retail store, they make money when you ship their rice pudding worldwide by ordering through their website, and they'll make a LOT of money franchising the concept.

Another way to put this is what Al Ries and Jack Trout call (in their book *Marketing Warfare*) "Principle 3: Launch the attack on as narrow a front as possible."

Be narrow—and go deep!

DO IT! YOUR DIVERSIFY-WHILE-STILL-SPECIALIZING GAME PLAN

What you currently do:
_____
_____

Whom you do it for:
_____
_____

How you do it:
_____
_____

Where you do it:
_____
_____

What else could you do?
_____
_____

For whom else?
_____
_____

How else could you do it?
_____
_____

Where else?
_____
_____

What's a crazy idea for specializing our current business?

_____

_____

What's a crazy idea for diversifying our current business?

_____

_____

Which of these ideas might be crazy enough to work?

_____

_____

Alternate strategy: Develop a second parallel offering/division/brand that taps into your unique expertise but appeals to different:

Industries:

_____

_____

Needs:

_____

_____

Audiences:

_____

_____

Niches:

_____

_____

Price points:

_____

_____

DO IT! SUCCESS STRATEGY: 11 WAYS TO OWN YOUR NICHE

Stephanie Chandler

As a business owner, entrepreneur, or independent professional, *you* have the rare opportunity to establish authority in your field, which makes it easier to stand out against competitors.

Ideally, you should have a multifaceted marketing strategy that includes sharing great content across multiple networks online.

Here are some ways to begin building your audience, promoting your brand, and claiming ownership of your niche.

1. Build an authoritative website: Your website should dazzle visitors, position you as an authority in your field, and be as professional as possible. If any of these elements are missing, it's time for a redesign.

2. Write a buzz-worthy blog: If you could do just one thing to market your business online, write a great blog. The blog is at the heart of everything you do in establishing yourself as an authority in your field. It's where you can communicate with readers and generate more web traffic. Update it several times each week, and share each new post across your social media networks.

3. Become a speaker: When you're the expert at the front of the room, people pay attention. Dazzle them, and they will want to buy your products and services.

4. Write a book: Becoming an author is a game changer. A book is the most impressive business card or brochure you can have. It will open doors—guaranteed.

5. Take a stand: If you want to stand out from your competitors, be yourself, not a clone of everyone else. Following so-called blueprints and proven formulas will get you only so far. If you really want to stand out, be who you are, and stand up for what you believe.

6. Mix up your media: Videos get a lot of action in Google search, and YouTube.com is one of the most searched sites in the world. How-to videos can be a great way for potential prospects to find you.

7. Develop information products: More than ever, we live in a society that consumes information. Create reports, white papers, workbooks, and e-books, and give them away liberally. That's right, give them away for free. You'll get results worth many times their value.

8. Do something unexpected: The Internet is full of things that have already been done in your own industry, so look outside the box for ideas. Could you host a virtual conference? Hold a fun contest with spectacular prizes? Give a free high-value Q&A chat each week?

9. Carve out creative time: It takes ideas to build a business, and if you're working so hard that you rarely come up for air or have a moment to think, you are killing your best ideas. Designate creative time during the week for brainstorming. That might mean getting out for a walk, sitting in a coffee shop, or locking yourself in a conference room for an afternoon. Whatever works for you is fine as long as you make it a priority.

10. Lead something: You can participate in networking groups all day, but when you lead a group, the earth shifts beneath your feet. Start an online group via LinkedIn or Facebook or launch a local group in your own backyard.

11. Rock your niche: You may not be the only person in your niche, but you can be the best at what you do in your own unique way. But you can't do this if you aren't staying on top of industry trends, experimenting, implementing, and trying new things. Go out and learn as much as you can and then teach others everything you know, and I mean everything. Give away your best material. Seriously. Although some will go off and try to do it on their own, many others will come back for more and want to buy whatever you're selling. Empower them with information, and you will build an extremely loyal audience.

Stephanie Chandler is the author of several books, including *Own Your Niche: Hype-Free Internet Marketing Tactics to Establish Authority in Your*

Field and Promote Your Service-Based Business. She is also CEO of http://AuthorityPublishing.com. specializing in custom book publishing and social media marketing services, and http://BusinessInfoGuide.com, a directory of resources for entrepreneurs. A frequent speaker at business events and on the radio, she has been featured in *Entrepreneur*, *BusinessWeek*, and *Wired*, and she is a blogger for *Forbes*.

✓ 63 FOCUS ON STRATEGY, NOT TACTICS

As a small business marketing coach, I've observed

that **strategic** business owners tend to be highly focused.

And overly **tactical** business owners tend to be scattered.

If you want lasting and profitable business success, the key is to marry a small number of highly focused strategies with a variety of tightly aligned marketing and sales and operational tactics.

Here are seven keys to help you get started. Use the spaces to answer some of these questions and to reflect on your own good advice.

1. Tactics are easy, and it's tempting to confuse executing tactics with moving your business forward. **How do you find yourself getting lost in the tactical weeds?**

_____

_____

_____

2. Strategy is the WHY TO and tactics are the HOW TO. If you stop focusing on your WHY, even for a short time, you'll fall into the trap of getting really good at creating and selling projects/services that you don't want to be doing. **How are you trapping yourself with off-strategy successes?**

_____

_____

_____

3. It _feels_ good to execute tactics, and it _feels_ hard to create strategies. This is because you have to come face-to-face with the time–space continuum. You can't execute everything you want to do all at once, and you probably shouldn't try. **How have you subconsciously let yourself be overwhelmed with not enough strategy but too many tactics?**

_____

_____

_____

4. Tactics pile up; there is always more to do. Strategy is a limiting factor. Strategy shows you what you should NOT be building, selling, and offering. Strategy serves your business as a filter. With no strategy, every tactic looks reasonable. **How have you buried yourself in tactics while starving yourself of strategy?**

_____

_____

_____

5. Business owners and entrepreneurs LOVE talking to each other about tactics. What's worked? What hasn't? What's next? They rarely talk strategy. They rarely talk about things they want to stop doing. **What questions could you ask your colleagues to find out what they have pared down and eliminated to help them increase their strategic focus?**

_____

_____

_____

6. "We're too busy for strategy." Really? How about escaping to a coffee shop for a morning with a notebook and a set of colored markers to have a strategic meeting with yourself? In less than two hours, you can do a data dump, a project review, a client review, and an ideal-business-model exercise. You can also create several lists, such as "Low-payoff activities that take too much of my time" and "High-payoff activities that I need to create more time for." Take your notes back to the office, summarize and categorize them, and begin to put them into action. **When's the last time you had a strategic meeting with yourself?**

_____

_____

_____

7. E-mail is not a strategy. E-mail is not a tactic. And e-mail is not a high-payoff activity. Yes, you might get a few important client e-mails a day or customer service e-mails or a handful of leads. Other than that, e-mail is a deadly distraction. So stop. Make a sign over your desk where you can see it from your computer that says, "E-MAIL IS NOT MY JOB." **How has e-mail stolen your strategic focus lately?**

_____

_____

_____

To download over 100 strategic AND tactical resources to help you organize your marketing, visit **www.doitmarketing.com/book.**

64 PLANNING TRUMPS PASSION EVERY TIME!

Passion is not enough. In other words, plan to fail.

Here's a big old *Fast Company*–style myth: Passion is the fuel of innovation, business, and success.

Nope. It's not. Passion is necessary but not sufficient.

Let me repeat that: Passion is necessary but not sufficient. Let's make an assumption: No matter how much passion you have, your big idea will fail. Then what?

People who have an attitude that "failure is not an option" have a failure rate about 49 percent higher than people who have a more realistic outlook. (I just made up that statistic—do you like it? Research shows that 81 percent of statistics are made up on the spot!)

When people account for failure, they develop a really strong plan B... and plan C and plans D, E, and F, too.

You're gonna have plenty of great ideas. I hope you will ACT ON many of them. But I'd be lying if I told you that you'll succeed at any one of them by passion alone. That's baloney.

Here's some space to make plans for your next glorious failure.

Planning for Failure Worksheet

Plan A was:

_____

_____

Plan B is:

_____

_____

Plan C will be:

_____

_____

Plan D will be:

_____

_____

If I need a plan E, it might be:

_____

_____

If all else fails, Plan F is:

_____

_____

The more you **think through failure**, **think ahead of failure**, and **think beyond failure**, the better your chances of ultimate success.
Remember the *Titanic*? It was unsinkable. They didn't plan to fail. So they did.

PART ELEVEN

PERSONAL
SUCCESS STRATEGIES

65 CONFIDENCE IS SEXY

"As is our confidence, so is our capacity."

—WILLIAM HAZLITT

"Confidence thrives on honesty, on honor, on the sacredness of obligations, and on unselfish performance. Without them it cannot live."

—FRANKLIN D. ROOSEVELT

CONFIDENCE 101

* What are you great at?
* How did you first learn it?
* How long did it take to become great at it?
* What was that learning process like?
* Who helped you along the way?
* How did you feel about that person?
* How can you pass along this skill or ability?
* Have you done so? Why or why not?
* Would you like to? Who comes to mind?
* How could you develop this skill further?
* Will you? Why or why not?
* What does this skill or capability give you?
* What else might you be great at?
* What could you start doing today (for fun) that might become the next thing you're great at?
* What questions come to mind when you think about being great at something?

- How have you answered those questions with the skill you're already great at?
- Did your questions change over time?
- What is your definition of greatness?
- Does confidence sometimes mean focusing on your game, not the external judgments of others?
- How can judgments and criticisms help you?
- How can they be harmful?
- Are they even important?

66 CHARM IS *NOT* A FOUR-LETTER WORD

"You know what charm is: a way of getting the answer 'Yes' without having asked any clear question."

—Albert Camus

A lot of independent professionals and business owners bristle at the notion that charm is a key business tool.

Much of that bristling comes from the misconception that some people are simply born with charm, while others are not, and that you can't do a whole lot about it if you're in that second group.

This is simply not true.

Another misconception is that, for the charm challenged, making any effort to be more charming or more personable would require them to be phony or, at best, not be their genuine selves. False again.

Several books—the best of which is *How to Connect in Business in 90 Seconds or Less* by Nicholas Boothman—offer great tools with which to make genuine connections with people and to build your own personal set of charm skills that apply in almost any business or social situation.

Let's face it: For the purposes of marketing and sales, people are buying YOU before they buy anything you have to sell, say, or do.

Question: Given the choice of boosting either your charm or your intellect by 50 percent, which would you choose?

Why?

Does the business world need more smart people or more charming people?

Haven't we gotten in trouble from people being (or thinking they were) too smart at companies like Enron, WorldCom, Tyco, AIG, Lehman Brothers, and the like?

Tip: Charm, like intelligence or any other personality strength, can be used for good or for evil. It's totally up to you.

Here are three ideas to help you boost your personal charm, likeability, and connection powers from Nick Boothman's book:

DO IT! CHARM SCHOOL

1. **Look people in the eye and smile.** Eye contact engenders trust. Smiling makes you appear happy and confident.
2. **Fit in—become a chameleon.** We feel comfortable with people who are like us. Match and mirror others' body language, their vocal tone and pace.
3. **Capture the imagination.** Use sensory-rich language and images so that others can see, hear, feel, and sometimes even smell and taste what you mean.

Now go charm the socks off someone!

67 LONE WOLVES STARVE TO DEATH

You need allies. You need partners. You need people willing and able to support your success as you support theirs.

Think about a wolf pack. Researchers in Estonia found that when wolves no longer lived, traveled, and hunted in packs (because too many pack leaders were being killed by hunters), the wolves had a much worse time of it.

Wolf researcher Enn Vilbaste says, "Loners are the worst—they don't have pack support to hunt down wild prey. So they come near the human settlements to kill dogs and other domestic animals."

Together—with support from other pack members—wolves can catch much bigger prey.

When on their own, they go after smaller domestic animals, and many starve. They always **do much better in a pack!**

Question: How do you collaborate?

* What approaches do you use?
* How can you get into meaningful alliances?
* How does communication play a role?
* What blocks you from collaborating?
* What happens when you allow allies get closer than you've let them in the past?

Tips to jump-start your thinking:

* Look for people who have partnered with others in the past, and ask them to tell you their stories
* Remember when you have been a helpful ally, and remind yourself you can do it
* Read books or articles about people who have partnered with another: Ben and Jerry, George and Gracie, Rogers and Hammerstein, Abbott and Costello
* Practice partnering on something very small, such as doubles tennis or team bowling
* Remember a time when you did something in a partnership that you thought you could never do alone
* Think of a time that you put a lot of trust in someone else to help you out, and they did!
* Notice whenever someone asks you for help or assistance in the smallest way
* Notice how often you naturally work in twos, threes, or fours to get something done (move furniture, hang a picture, row a canoe)

☑ 68 LIVE OUT OF YOUR CALENDAR NOT YOUR INBOX

Ever had a truly high-output day where you felt super-productive, not only with your marketing and sales and business development tasks, but with every aspect of your life?

Want more of those days?

Sure you do! By the time you're done reading this chapter, you will have the secrets to creating your OWN high-payoff productivity burst any time you wish. But it takes more than wishing; it takes resolve and action.

Hint: It is simple but not easy.

What made that high-output day so special? Imagine having a day when:

🌟 You get **IMPORTANT** stuff done
🌟 You have more **FOCUS**
🌟 You **FEEL** better about what you accomplished
🌟 And you **ACCOMPLISH** more of what really matters to you and your business

In fact, it's very possible you accomplished more on that high-output day than on the four other days in that week combined!

The key: Get a better handle on what your key high-payoff activities TRULY are. Then put them on your calendar in specific time slots. And the screen that should be under your nose all day is your CALENDAR, not your e-mail INBOX.

QUICK TIPS

1. Plan your day: What MUST get done and WHEN?
2. Chunk your day down into blocks, and assign specific tasks to those blocks: phone calls, e-mails, client tasks, whatever it is YOU want to do that will move you closer to your GOALS.
3. Keep that damn calendar under your nose. All day. Make it your default screen. Hide, minimize, or (gasp) close your e-mail until "Check e-mail" pops up on your calendar.
4. Make a note of COMPLETING your high-payoff activities. Checkmark them on your task list or change their color on your calendar so that you have a visual roadmap of achievement for your day.

So what's the big deal? What did I get done on my high-output day?

1. Had a coaching call with one of my awesome clients in Canada
2. Answered a LinkedIn message from a new prospect[*]
3. Followed up with FIVE key prospects by sending a high-value article on referrals
4. Wrote this section of the book
5. Connected with a client for an upcoming Do It! Marketing Seminar
6. Followed up with an editor of a financial publication about doing a podcast and speaking at several of their conferences.
7. Took care of some billing nonsense that I've been putting off for two weeks. (I hate that stuff, thus keeping my bookkeeper and accountant profitably busy!)
8. Made one important prospecting phone call (the only thing I hate more than financial detail work is using the phone.)
9. Connected with my Vistage Chair to ask him an important favor
10. Got a solid "no" from a prospect on the phone and ended the prospecting/sales process with her on a strong positive note. (Did I mention how much I hate the damn phone? Gotta use it, though.)

All together, I had 10 high-payoff activities on my calendar and knocked all of them out before 3 p.m. Changed their colors, made follow-up notes, and felt great about the results of the day.

The short lesson: Live by your calendar, NOT by your inbox!

Note: You may have noticed that my second item was to respond to a LinkedIn e-mail. I was able to do that because I did a Money Pass through my e-mail inbox, and the new prospect inquiry from LinkedIn qualified as a MONEY-MAKING ACTIVITY, so I proactively added it to my day in real time. (See more about the Money Pass in the next chapter.)

69 FIVE WAYS TO USE E-MAIL WITHOUT GETTING SUCKED IN

Like you, I struggle with e-mail.

You probably find yourself:

- Getting too much e-mail (duh!)
- Spending too much time on e-mail
- Getting sucked into long sessions of e-mail reactionary time (aka swatting e-mail flies)
- Confusing your all-important business productivity with the amount of e-mail you read, reply to, and process in a day
- Wondering what happened to all those high-priority, money-making tasks that you promised yourself you'd get done today

E-mail is simply a reality of how you do business, how you serve your clients, and how you make a living.

And you're probably like most business owners, entrepreneurs, and independent professionals in that **you've tried dozens of ways to loosen the grip that e-mail has on you day and night**—at your computer, on your smartphone, on your iPad, and even in your brain cells.

That's right: E-mail is even stuck in your brain. C'mon, admit it. You've had dreams about your inbox. Sad but true. There's no shame in it, and you're definitely not alone!

Occasionally (mostly on weekends), I make a commitment to stay OFF e-mail.

Bad news: It usually doesn't work.

Good news: I found five great workarounds for USING e-mail without getting SUCKED IN.

Here are the five specific strategies you can use to laser-target your e-mail activity and get some important things done in five minutes or less **without the distraction** of looking at the hundreds of messages hopelessly piling up by the minute in your inbox:

1. TARGETED SEARCH

Use your e-mail program's search feature proactively when you want to find something in particular. Example: I recall getting an e-mail from Staples that I had some Rewards bucks that were going to expire soon. I jumped into the search box, typed "Staples.com" and in 60 seconds, I was printing out my discount coupons and on my merry way to the Staples website and AWAY from my inbox! Like an e-mail commando: quick in, quick out.

2. SEND FROM THE HIP

On a different Saturday, I wanted to send a quick note to a client about our next appointment. Your usual routine is probably like mine; we send from the inbox screen. And there are ALL those distracting messages clamoring for our attention.

It doesn't have to be that way.

This time, I opened my e-mail and immediately hit the Compose button. The new blank e-mail filled my screen. I addressed the e-mail, popped in my subject line, typed out a short note to my client, hit send, and immediately closed out of e-mail. Like an e-mail ninja: silent but deadly!

3. RAPID REPLY

Ever get that nagging feeling that you have some unfinished e-mail business, but you just can't quite remember what it is? Then it hits you in the middle of the night: Reply to Bob about his pricing question! So you pad downstairs at 2 a.m., sit down in front of your e-mail, and pretty soon it's 4 a.m. because you got sucked in.

It's not unusual for folks to spend 2 hours on e-mail, get up from their desk, and realize that they forgot the original e-mail issue that they sat down to take care of in the first place. Yikes!

Here's the answer, and it builds on the Targeted Search technique. First, search for Bob's e-mail address. If you can't remember it, search for his company name, the word "pricing," or anything else you recall from your last e-mail exchange. Your search results should fill your screen and replace the inbox view.

Once you find the e-mail in question, hit reply, compose your answer, attach any needed documents, and close out of e-mail.

The goal is to reply rapidly without looking at your inbox contents. If you do catch a glimpse, deploy some self-control and consciously do not LOOK at your inbox contents for the few seconds they may be visible on your screen. (Good job!)

4. DEEP DIG

I wanted to find a specific Wikipedia tip that I remembered was buried in an e-mail newsletter I receive. This newsletter is one of about half a dozen that I've subscribed to for years and read regularly. The content is so good that I keep most of the back issues in an e-mail folder I call Research.

When I sat down to find this tip, I did NOT want to get sucked into e-mail. So, again, my starting place was the Targeted Search technique. But because these newsletters are so content packed, I needed to search the body text of the e-mails that came up in the search results. Also, because I knew this e-mail was in my Research folder, I limited my search to that location.

I tried searching for "Wikipedia," only to realize that this newsletter editor frequently references that site for additional info on the topics that she covers. Then I searched for a few more keywords and short phrases. Finally, I remembered the person who submitted the tip and used the search criteria in combination with his name. Bingo! Two entries found: one from 2009 and one from 2011. The older one contained the gem I was looking for.

Did I spend some deep-dig research time? Yes, indeed. Did I waste any time getting SUCKED INTO e-mail hell? Nope. And you won't either if you stay focused.

5. DO A MONEY PASS

This final technique specifically combats getting sucked into e-mail. Suppose you have a backlog of e-mails waiting in your inbox (for example, my count right now is 226 because I wanted to write this chapter before getting sucked into e-mail!) When that happens, you need to put on your money goggles.

With those money goggles firmly secured over your eyeballs, go bravely forth into your inbox. Ruthlessly ask yourself this question over and over as you survey your inbox contents: "Will replying to this e-mail make me money?"

For example:

- Is it from a current paying client?
- Is it from an active prospect moving through your sales process?
- Is it from a past client who has paid you money?
- Is it a referral or other note from one of your advocates, allies, or partners?
- Is it a new lead or opportunity to sell more products, services, or programs?

Once you do your Money Pass, you can relegate the rest of your e-mail processing to some downtime or other non-peak admin time.

As my friend, e-mail productivity expert Marsha Egan, says, "E-mail is not your job." (Her e-mail management principles pretty much saved my life. See www.InboxDetox.com to see what I mean.)

E-mail is NOT your job. Put that up on your wall where you can see it clearly from your computer! It is a VERY big insight, if you ask me.

Using these five strategies plus some intentionally applied willpower, which will come more easily as you use them, you will take back control of your time, your day, and your life!

So close your email and get all the free marketing tools, templates, and business growth resources waiting for you at **www.doitmarketing.com/ book.**

☑ 70 THE SECRET SAUCE

Want to know the secret sauce to your success?

You ready? Here's the hidden formula, what separates the men from the boys and the women from the girls, the magic bullet for success in any field:

Stamina.

Success means you've got a long road ahead of you. And either you have the rocket fuel of originality, passion, purpose, and love, or you have the rather lame motivator of money. Which do you think will last longer in that race?

Stamina is utterly important. And stamina is possible only if it's managed well.

In 1999, when I was sharing my big plans for launching my business at a dinner with some longtime friends, one of them asked me, "But how are you going to build a business like that?" Another friend wisely and quietly offered these words of wisdom: "He's going to do it one client at a time."

A common theme I hear from my clients when we start to ramp up their marketing and sales efforts—doing research, doing intelligent prospecting, coming up with remarkable products and services, focusing on narrow niche markets—is, "But David, that's a lot of work." Welcome to the world of marketing, sales, and global domination.

This is a marathon, not a sprint, and you have to have the stamina for it.

Tom Peters said, "The key to success in business is surviving long enough to get lucky."

☑ 71 DO *WHAT* YOU LOVE FOR *PEOPLE* YOU LOVE

"All you need is love."
—The Beatles

One of the most powerful business tools for entre-preneurs and executives is self-knowledge. Use your self-knowledge to unleash the power of love in your business—to do what you love for people you love.

In the simplest terms, unleashing the power of love comes down to answering these basic questions:

- ✳ Who am I?
- ✳ What am I all about?
- ✳ What do I love to do?
- ✳ Who do I want to be?
- ✳ What's the best way for me to get there?
- ✳ Where would I like the journey to take me?

Here is a simple model for bringing together your highest self with your best work and your perfect customers. Consider these three circles:

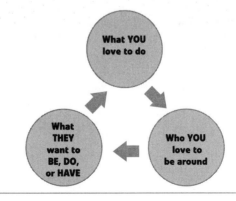

Spend a few moments answering the following questions.

Your Best Self, Your Best Work, and Your Perfect Customers

1. **WHAT you love to do:** List all the professional pursuits, activities, and interests you love.

_____

_____

_____

2. **WHO you love to be around:** List the types of people you enjoy spending time with.

_____

_____

_____

3. **What THEY want to BE, DO, and HAVE:** Connect to the core wants, needs, desires, dreams and aspirations with the folks in Question 2 by providing them with something you're naturally great at from Question 1, and you'll create a passionate, profitable and practical business.

_____

_____

_____

DO IT! 10 ACTIVITIES YOU LOVE TO DO

Any context is fine. Use your personal life, professional life, life with your family, friends, civic and religious groups—anything:

1. _____
2. _____

3. _____

4. _____

5. _____

6. _____

7. _____

8. _____

9. _____

10. _____

Now review your list and summarize each of these 10 items into a one-word VERB, such as "teach" or "analyze" or "cultivate."

These are 10 of your core action words that define you at your best.

How can you create more opportunities to use these actions? In answering this question, please remember that even a small change can have a huge impact.

You don't need to quit your job in an office in New York and move to a kibbutz in Israel if one of your key words turned out to be "share." You can share some of what you know with your colleagues. Teach a class, write an article, start a discussion group, create a lunchtime seminar series, or start an online forum for your customers and prospects. So many entrepreneurs and executives are unhappy because the opportunities to use these core actions have evaporated from their lives or have become blocked by schedules filled with too much to do and never enough time.

But stop and ask yourself, "How effective is my mind if my heart and soul are starving?"

And if you don't take care of them, who will?

PART TWELVE

TAKING ACTION

☑ **72** FIVE MARKETING MOVES FOR BUSINESS SUCCESS

Marketing has traditionally been broken down to a formula known as the Five P's, the five factors that make up your marketing strategy. If these are done consistently, well, and for a long enough period of time, they become part of your brand.

So far, so good.

But the problem is that no one can seem to agree on exactly which Five P's are important, so the list typically includes people, product, place, process, price, promotion, paradigm, perspective, persuasion, passion, positioning, packaging, and performance.

Wow. Sounds complicated, huh?

Let's simplify: All you need are five marketing moves—five concrete actions—that you can **implement immediately.**

Your challenge: Try one or more of these NOW.

☑ **73** MOVE UP

Want to try something different? The next time you're speaking with a prospect, when the question of price comes up, quote DOUBLE your normal price and see what happens.

Risky? Maybe. A good test? For sure.

Why? **Because you'll find out if maybe YOU'RE not charging enough for your value, but instead you're competing on price.**

Businesses that compete on price lose. Period.

The easiest thing your competition can do is undercut your price. In fact, the first thing they will copy is your price. It takes no imagination, no creativity, no innovation, no market leadership, and no vision to lower the cost of something. And it hurts all parties involved. Lower prices always mean lower profits. Studies have shown that a 1 percent drop in price leads to an 8 percent drop in profit.

DO IT! DOUBLING YOUR PRICE

Is this crazy? Maybe. Maybe not.

Several things will happen, all of them good. Your prospects will perceive:

* An increase in the **value** of your product/service
* An increased level of **prestige** in owning or using your product/service
* An increased level of **trust** in you and your offerings (the halo effect)
* An increased level of **confidence** that your product/service really works

A client, who happened to be a marketing consultant herself, once gave me a very valuable piece of advice: **"Be expensive or be free."** Being one of the most expensive providers of a service is remarkable. People talk about $1.3 million sports cars and $21,000 platinum-plated, diamond-studded cell phones (even if they never buy one). Nobody talks about a $23,000 GM sedan.

Several of my client companies have doubled their prices, with great success, and several more of my solopreneurs clients have doubled (and in one case tripled) their fees. In each of those cases, they got more clients, not fewer.

Perhaps you'll lose a few unprofitable clients along the way. If you don't lose some unprofitable clients, you won't have room to serve the more profitable ones when they come along.

It's professional suicide to continue focusing on serving a market sector that can afford to pay your old (low) prices. Price doesn't find clients. Value finds clients. And clients who value your work should—and will—pay according to that value.

Free is also a powerful price point. And, of course, free has a certain wow factor too, but only if you give away what other companies would normally charge for.

Let me repeat that because it's so vitally important:

> **FREE has meaning only if you give away what other companies would normally charge for.**

You move up when you **give VALUE first**.

Got a great idea for your prospects? Great! SEND IT TO THEM.

Even better, got a business lead for them? Hand it over!

Did you come across an article or a piece of research that impacts their business? Clip it and mail it to the CEO with a brief note.

That prospect's door is now open. And you are now ready to move UP!

74 MOVE IN

Moving in means moving closer to your customers.

We already talked about the power of living in your prospects' world, thinking about their problems, and thinking about their clients and prospects.

Don't like sitting at the computer all day? Then you'll love this assignment:

DO IT! HIT THE STREETS!

Visit some prospects, pop into local businesses, talk to your contacts in the fields you serve, get some firsthand information about what's going on in their world.

What are their challenges, heartaches, headaches, opinions, obstacles, priorities?

What are their dreams, their if-only's, and their biggest aspirations?

What solutions, services, and answers are they seeking now—today—right this very minute?

Take these folks out for breakfast, lunch, coffee, drinks, dinner.

Don't sell them anything. Ask questions, shut up, and LISTEN!

Is this a lot of work? You bet.

Do the majority of your competitors put in this kind of effort? No way.

That is exactly why **YOU** should.

✓ **75** MOVE AHEAD

Moving ahead means going above and beyond

what most business owners and professionals are doing.

It means putting in the work—yes, the really hard work—that makes the difference between being a peddler and being a partner.

You can move ahead by charging more (remember moving up?) and by DEMONSTRATING the VALUE of your product service with hard numbers.

In his insightful book, *How to Become a Rainmaker*, author Jeffrey Fox calls this process dollarizing.

Dollarizing is one of the most powerful sales techniques because once you show the return on investment (with real numbers that your prospect will provide)—how THIS much spent will generate THIS much savings, or profits, or sales, or new clients, or hours, and the like—you basically shift the conversation from selling what you're selling to SELLING MONEY.

The Money Machine exercise will help you spell this out very clearly in hard dollars.

The Money Machine goes one step further because you can use it to dollarize against:

* Competing products/services
* The prospect doing nothing
* The prospect doing it themselves
* Other things the prospect is already comfortable spending money on

THE MONEY MACHINE WORKSHEET

According to sales expert and author Jeffrey Fox, Dollarization is the tangible, logical translation of your product or service claims (e.g., "safest," "most reliable," "longer life," "best deal," "superior quality," and so on) into dollars and cents.

You can dollarize almost any benefit or point of difference for any product or service you sell. It takes some planning, thinking, and, in some cases, some specific numbers provided by your prospect.

Example: Faster insurance software = faster.

- The faster software saves 15 seconds of operator time for every claims transaction
- 15 seconds × 100 transactions a day × 70 claims processors = 29 work hours/day saved
- At $40/hour total wages (salary + benefits + overhead) per claims processor 29 hours × $40 = $1,160 a day savings, or $5,800 per week, or **$290,000** a year
- Cost of new insurance software system = $150,000
- Total time to payback = 6 months. Total savings thereafter = $5,800/week

You can even dollarize against competing products/services. You can dollarize against alternate courses of action (not doing anything or doing it yourself). And you can dollarize against your prospect's buying other, comfortable and familiar types of products or services.

Do this right, and suddenly your product/service becomes a real investment. You can show people the math behind putting this much IN for this much OUT. You've earned the right to move ahead.

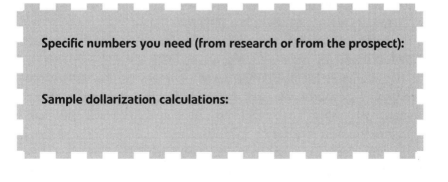

Specific numbers you need (from research or from the prospect):

Sample dollarization calculations:

76 MOVE ASIDE

Here's another thing that most small business

owners, entrepreneurs, and professionals have a hard time with:
You can't be all things to all people.

Moving aside is about finding your niche and claiming your expertise in a narrow area of specialty.

In plain English, this means you want to become the go-to guy or gal for your specific product or service—the exact opposite of a being jack-of-all-trades and master of none.

The people you speak with will have a very different reaction to these two mental images of your product/service:

"I thi-i-i-ink this might solve our problem"
versus
"This is exactly what we've been looking for!"
Here's an example.

A company near my home in suburban Philadelphia lists among its services "Carpet Removal, House Cleaning, Odd Jobs, Catering."

Now, I don't know about you, but when I want a caterer, I'm looking for someone who does catering 24/7. I don't want to have to worry about whether they washed their hands after the carpet removal job and before serving my guests.

In fact, if I'm looking for a caterer for a wedding, I might even be drawn to Wedding Bells Catering much more so than Sam's Catering or Good Eats Catering.

Here's another example. I meet owners of many graphic design firms who do all sorts of work—websites, logo design, brochures, collateral material, wine labels, book packaging, and so on. You name it, they do it. And their business is generally doing OK. (Then again, if they were going like gangbusters, they probably wouldn't have sought out my help!)

Some of them have a hard time differentiating themselves from the competition and others find it challenging to develop a strong client base and referral network.

They've had some good success developing their current business. Yet when we delve into the possibility of moving aside and carving out a real niche or developing one thing that is their flagship specialty, most of my clients get cold feet.

One company (not my client—too bad for me!) that has done this with fabulous results is MaxEffect. They made a tough call. They moved aside.

They could do a wide variety of things with their graphic design and advertising skills, but they do ONE THING: They work exclusively on *Yellow Pages* ads.

That's it.

If you want a killer *Yellow Pages* ad with bold graphics, custom or stock photography, clean layout, and a strong, compelling message, they are your go-to people.

They've designed hundreds and hundreds of *Yellow Pages* ads, and they've built a fanatical client base. They get a steady stream of referrals, not to mention the growing flow of client work.

Check it out for yourself: http://www.max-effect.com.

77 MOVE ALONE

Right now, you and your business are lost in a sea

of gray. Me-too rules the day. Everywhere you look, there is more and more and MORE of the SAME OLD THING sold by the SAME OLD PEOPLE in the SAME OLD WAY.

Boring.

And deadly.

The problem is that people don't buy gray.

If you and your company and your offerings blend into the background, you might as well close up shop right now.

Let me put it another way: All companies go bankrupt. It's just a matter of time.

Want proof? Out of the 100 largest companies of 50 years ago, 17 survive today. And none of those 17 are the market leaders they used to be.

Why? Shift happens. If you're not separating yourself from the crowd, you're blending in, and nobody will even notice you, much less seek you out and tell their friends about you.

Here's an example of a company that really hasn't been doing a bad job, but they're also not the standouts they used to be.

On a recent call to a large credit-card-issuing bank, I was straightening out a billing problem. At the end of the call, the operator asked me, "Have I exceeded your expectations for this call?" and I flatly answered, "No." I had a billing problem, and the rep fixed it. **That's my expectation.**

Now, if the rep had offered me a $50 gift card, THAT would have exceeded expectations, right? That story would be worth repeating to 10–20 people. Can you imagine telling someone, "Hey, I called the bank to fix my billing error. Guess what? They fixed it!" That's not moving alone.

Here's a good test to see whether your marketing and sales strategies are in the category of moving alone. They are if you're doing something that:

* Is simply not done in your industry
* Customers can't help telling their friends about
* Goes against conventional wisdom (uncommon sense)
* Others (including your competition) think is "crazy"
* Others (including your competition) will actually be AFRAID to copy

Get silly. Get crazy. Get an attitude. Get noticed.

Author Seth Godin perhaps put this most succinctly when he said, "Safe is risky. And risky is safe."

Here's a recap of the Five Marketing Moves so you have them handy:

1. **Move Up:** Get more valuable
2. **Move In:** Get closer
3. **Move Ahead:** Get smarter

4. **Move Aside:** Get specialized
5. **Move Alone:** Get noticed

Taken together, these will also help you make the ultimate move, as Apple founder Steve Jobs coined the term: **Get insanely great.**

Photo courtesy of Denys Prykhodov/Shutterstock.com

And remember the immortal words of Jerry Garcia: **"You don't want to be considered the best of the best. You want to be considered the only ones who do what you do."**

For tools, resources, and downloads to help you implement these five marketing moves in your business (plus a whole bunch of other business building bonuses and special gifts), visit **www.doitmarketing.com/book.**

DO IT! SUCCESS STRATEGY: FOUR MORE MOVES THAT MATTER

Scott Ginsberg

Entrepreneurs and executives like you are smart.

You've mastered marketing, sales, leadership, operations, and customer service.

Occasionally, you might forget the basic elements that make you successful. And to ignore them is to ignore your potential to win new business.

Key thought: Business owners who make smart, small moves, win.

Consider adding these four into your daily mix:

1. Create memorability. These nine words are worth repeating: "Thank you for allowing me to learn something today." That was the exit line by the customer service agent of Bank of America. Not, "Thank you for calling." Not, "Is there anything else I can do for you?" Not, "Are you satisfied with your level of service today?" Not, "Would you be willing to take a minute to answer our online survey about your customer experience for the chance to win a thousand dollars?" Just, "Thank you." In his gratitude, he demonstrated respect. In his ignorance, he projected vulnerability. In his unexpectedness, he created memorability. **Can you or your service team do all that in nine words?**

2. Sell what's possible. Ever been to Lifetime Fitness? These facilities are a marvel of modern exercise. Consider the amenities: two lap pools; concert-quality cycling theater; four hardwood basketball courts; multiple machine options for each body part; one hundred thousand square feet of exercise space; hundreds of cardio choices with no waiting, guaranteed. Sound excessive? Sound wasteful? Maybe. But at the gym, it's not that we need it, it's that it's possible. And we will always pay for possibility. Lifetime doesn't sell fitness; they sell hope. Lots of it. **What do you sell?**

3. Practice consistency. When we tell our story the same way, all the time, everywhere, people don't just buy from us once, they join with us forever. Stay at any Ritz-Carlton around the globe, and the employees offer the same warm welcome, deliver the same anticipatory service, and embody the same attitude. Take a class at any Bikram Yoga Studio around the world, and the instructors will use the same language, teach the same postures, and practice the same philosophy. Fly Virgin Air to any city around the world, and the flight crew will have the same casual demeanor, the same friendly nuance, and the same attractive design. Same, same, same. It's the four-letter word people expect from us in the future. **Where is your consistency?**

4. Sign everything. I recently talked to a woman who designed her own wedding gown. When I saw a picture of the dress, I asked where she planned to sign it. After all, it truly was a stunning work of art. She said hadn't given it much thought. Funny. I tend to give these things a lot of thought. Seems to me, if we don't sign it, why ship it? A crucial part of being an artist is signing our work—taking pride in our creations and putting our name on them for people to see. It's not narcissism or shameless self-promotion. And it's not born out of some kind of artistic insecurity. It's simply part of the job description: taking accountability for our art. When we express ourselves, there's nothing wrong with signing a name on the self we express. **What's your signature?**

Scott Ginsberg is the only person who wears a name tag 24/7. More importantly, he's the only person in the world who made a career out of wearing a name tag 24/7. As the author of 21 books, a professional speaker, an award-winning blogger, and the producer of NametagTV.com, Scott's publishing and consulting company specializes in approachability, identity, and execution.

He's been featured on every major news outlet in the country, including *The Wall Street Journal*, *USA Today*, *NPR*, *MSNBC*, *Fast Company*—and, even wrote a quiz for *Cosmo* magazine. When he's not traveling around the world giving speeches, Scott lives in Brooklyn, where he often talks to strangers.

PART THIRTEEN

YOUR 21-DAY
MARKETING
LAUNCH PLAN

Now it's time to get you into action—step by step and day by day.

You may be brand new and just starting your business, or you may be a seasoned business owner who has been running your company for 10, 15, or even 20 years.

This **21-Day Launch Plan** will work for you no matter where you find yourself in your business. Visit **www.doitmarketing.com/book** to download your 21-Day Do It! Marketing Playbook to define, organize, implement, and track your marketing activities, tasks, and milestones in order to keep your marketing momentum moving forward and generating results week after week, month after month.

Each day of this **21-Day Launch Plan,** you'll get a specific assignment, task, or miniproject to complete. Nothing is left out, nothing is assumed, nothing is left to chance. This program is simple but not simplistic.

Day by day, you'll build everything you need: honing your message, targeting high-probability prospects, social media, e-mail marketing, building out your website as a marketing magnet, and dozens of other topics, tasks, and tools.

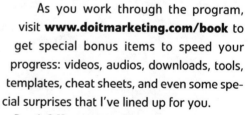

As you work through the program, visit **www.doitmarketing.com/book** to get special bonus items to speed your progress: videos, audios, downloads, tools, templates, cheat sheets, and even some special surprises that I've lined up for you.

Ready? **Here we go!**

DAY 1:
WHO ARE *YOU*?

Take some time to answer these questions, or jot some detailed notes for further thought. Complete this now, and you'll gain some clarity around these BIG questions. You'll be ready to make good decisions about the future direction of your marketing—and your business.

ACTIVITY:
DEFINE AND DECIDE

YOUR BUSINESS MODEL

Are you building:

- An organization (employees, sales force, offices, etc.)
- A practice (solo professional, no employees, work from home, etc.)
- A project-based consultancy (a loose affiliation of people and resources)
- Something that isn't any of these

YOUR REVENUE MODEL

How will you make money? How much and from what sources?

DO YOU WANT ACTIVE INCOME FROM:

- Selling products
- Selling services
- Selling expertise
- Short-term projects (less than 1 month)
- Medium-term projects (1–3 months)
- Long-term projects (3 months to 1 year or more)

DO YOU WANT PASSIVE INCOME FROM:

- ☀ **Memberships**
- ☀ **Information products (e-books, audios, videos, online resources)**
- ☀ **Affiliate programs**
- ☀ **Referral fees**
- ☀ **Licensing**
- ☀ **What else**

YOUR DELIVERY MODEL

How will you deliver your products, services, and value to your end customer?

DO YOU WANT TO FOCUS BY GEOGRAPHY?

- ☀ **Local**
- ☀ **Regional**
- ☀ **National**
- ☀ **International**

DO YOU WANT TO FOCUS BY METHOD?

- ☀ **In person**
- ☀ **Virtual (e-mail, phone, web)**
- ☀ **Retail**
- ☀ **Wholesale**
- ☀ **Franchisees**
- ☀ **Dealers**
- ☀ **Distributors**
- ☀ **Independent reps**

DO YOU WANT TO FOCUS ON CERTAIN MARKETS?

- ☀ **Business to Business (B2B)**
- ☀ **Business to Consumer (B2C)**
- ☀ **Industry specific**
- ☀ **Size specific (by annual revenue, number of employees, number of locations)**

DAY 2:
WHO ARE *THEY*?

Yesterday, we focused on identifying your business model, revenue model, and delivery model.

Today, we connect the dots from WHO you are (and WHAT you do) to the tribe of people (buyers, clients, audiences, professions) whom you wish to serve. This process is trickier than you may think. But you MUST laser-target YOUR peeps—the ones who don't need convincing. The ones who resonate with you TODAY. The ones who are actively SEEKING exactly what you offer. These are the buyers you want to work with the most because your expertise serves them the best.

In basic terms, today you'll decide on your target market: the group of potential clients you're trying to attract.

They're the people you hope will eventually hire you, buy from you, and become your customers and clients (and those you'll target with all of your marketing efforts).

Note: Don't panic or shy away from this exercise. You will NOT be "leaving money on the table." The sound bite is, "Target what you want, and you can always take what comes."

Begin this morning by taking some time to answer the Seven Buyer Persona Questions. Allow at least 60 minutes for this activity alone; it's THAT important!

ACTIVITY:
UNDERSTANDING YOUR BUYER PERSONA(S)

1. Think about your best clients and customers. WHAT makes them your best?
2. What are their job titles? Industries? Affiliations? Traits?
3. What problems do they have? What solutions do they SEEK? (in their own words)?
4. Where else have they looked previously?
5. Why hasn't that worked for them?

Spend the rest of the day revisiting those questions and refining them through research on targeted industry and association websites, forums, and blogs populated by members of your buyer persona. Allow 60–90 minutes for research time—you'll be glad you did!

If you're not sure what some of those are, simply use Google and enter search terms replacing the appropriate placeholders:

- [Your industry/expertise] website
- [Your industry/expertise] forum
- [Your industry/expertise] blog
- [Your industry/expertise] magazine
- [Your industry/expertise] newsletter

and/or:

- [Your target market] website
- [Your target market] forum
- [Your target market] blog
- [Your target market] magazine
- [Your target market] newsletter

Once you gain a "working vocabulary" from this research, refine your seven questions and clone their language in your answers. Focus on your target market's challenges, obstacles, and problems in their own words. (Allow 30 minutes to revise your seven answers using your new insights and specific BUYER language).

Enjoy a fun evening and a good night's rest after your excellent work today!

DAY 3:
DEVELOP YOUR PLATFORM-BUILDING PLAN—PART I

A platform-building plan is a combination marketing plan/visibility plan that you'll use throughout the rest of this program (and beyond).

Why do you want to create one? Because it will serve as your blueprint, showing you how to build an effective thought leadership platform that will attract the attention of the right kind of people—the people you want to market to. It includes:

* Your Budget (for Marketing/Client Acquisition)
* Your Niche
* Your Competition
* Your Strengths/Assets
* Your Obstacles/Blind Spots
* Your Marketing Language Bank (including Pain/Gain Factors)
* Your "Indisputable Points of Proof"
* Your Goals (Clients, Dollars, Revenue, Projects)
* Your Strategies
* Your Tactics (How? When? How often? Who does them?)

We'll tackle the first half of these tasks today and the rest tomorrow. You'll want to allow one or two hours for today's tasks. I don't recommend working straight through. Rather, set aside 30- to 60-minute blocks to give yourself breaks between your mental sprints!

Here's today's breakdown.

Your Budget (for Marketing and Client Acquisition)

For now, think about a monthly number that makes sense for a simple marketing budget. Zero is typically NOT a great answer. This doesn't need to be a lot, but you do need to start with something. Professional memberships cost money. Going to industry meetings costs money. Paying a web designer for a basic website costs money. You get the idea. How much can you set aside each month for a marketing fund? And it's obviously OK if you don't end up spending it in a given month. But it's better to have it and not need it than to need it and not have it!

Your Niche

You can focus and niche your expertise in several ways. The one that comes to mind for most business owners right away is to niche by target market (for example, marketing to dentists). And that would be ONE way to go, but there are many paths up the mountain! Let's explore the target market niche, and then you'll see a handful of others if this one doesn't fit your specific business.

Target market niche: Let's say you're a financial advisor. That's a good start. People know that you help them manage their money and investments wisely.

Let's do a deeper target market niche:

1. Financial advisor = good
2. Financial advisor for dentists = better
3. Financial advisor for dentists near retirement = best
4. Financial advisor for dentists near retirement who want to pay zero taxes = WOW!

That's a four-level niche! Going this deep makes your work repeatable and referable; people can easily repeat exactly what you do (and for WHOM) and refer that value proposition to others.

Here are other ways to carve your niche.

If niching by target market doesn't fit for your business, fear not! You can also niche:

* By functional area (for example, do you sell to HR people, finance people, IT people?)
* By industry (for example, banking, construction, health care)
* By level (senior execs, high school students, or first-time supervisors)
* By method (onsite, offsite, virtual, remote, on-demand, in person, etc.)
* By media (perhaps you're known for THE podcast, THE e-zine, or THE blog in your specific area of expertise)

The bottom line: This isn't necessarily hard to do, but only you can make these DECISIONS. Today is the day to start deciding.

Your Competition

For both a reality check and to learn how you might zig where the competition zags, spend some time surveying the competitive landscape of other businesses and professionals in your product/service arena. A quick Google search should turn up several viable competitors—locally, regionally, and nationally.

Once you've located between five to seven competitors, study how they present their value proposition. What do they say, and how do they say it? What's the secret sauce they're offering to their buyers and decision makers? Capture as much information about them today in the form of notes, short phrases, and key concepts or sound bites (and save the web links you find for future reference).

Your Strengths and Assets

Given the platform you want to build, it's important to know your own strengths and assets. These could be your own personality traits, your professional network, your "low-hanging-fruit" clients and prospects, your strong media connections, anything. Jot down three to five factors that put the wind at your back and that will make your professional life easier.

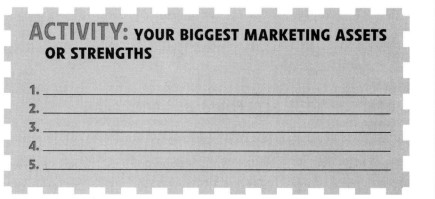

ACTIVITY: YOUR BIGGEST MARKETING ASSETS OR STRENGTHS

1. _____
2. _____
3. _____
4. _____
5. _____

Your Obstacles and Blind Spots

Equally important to your platform-building plan is identifying what stands in your way or where you feel you might need some outside perspective or support. Obstacles are challenges or weaknesses that you've identified. We're not going to dwell on the negative, although it is vitally important to KNOW yourself so that you can manage your way around weaknesses or blind spots and not let them derail your business success. Again, focus on identifying three to five of these for right now.

ACTIVITY:

YOUR BIGGEST MARKETING OBSTACLES OR BLIND SPOTS

1. _____
2. _____
3. _____
4. _____
5. _____

That's it for today. We'll tackle part II tomorrow, but until then, relax. You've earned it!

DAY 4:
DEVELOP YOUR PLATFORM-BUILDING PLAN— PART II

Yesterday, you did some fine work fleshing out the first part of your platform-building plan. Today, we'll complete your initial game plan by working on:

* Your Marketing Language Bank (including Pain/Gain Factors)
* Your "Indisputable Points of Proof"

- ☀ Your Goals (Clients, Projects, Revenue, Profit)
- ☀ Your Strategies (What are you committed to doing?)
- ☀ Your Tactics (How? When? Frequency? Who does them?)

Like yesterday, you'll want to allow one to two hours for today's tasks. Again, I don't recommend working straight through. Rather, set aside 30- to 60-minute blocks to give yourself breaks between your mental sprints!

Here's today's breakdown.

Your Marketing Language Bank (including Pain/Gain Factors)

On Day 2, you spent some time answering your Seven Buyer Persona Questions. This is the first half of your Marketing Language Bank. Good news: You're halfway done with this one already!

We spent considerable time in Chapter 12 exploring WHY a Marketing Language Bank is so critically vital to your success. You may want to flip back to that part of the book, review it, and then come back here. ...

Welcome back!

Here's the final part of your Marketing Language Bank—building your Pain/Gain Factors.

ACTIVITY:
YOUR BUYER'S PAIN/GAIN FACTORS

At this stage, take each of your selling points/features/benefits and REVERSE them so that each is positioned as pain relief, problem resolution, and nightmare prevention.

Remember to use real client language (in their own words), not marketing speak.

Refer to Chapter 15 to see an example you can model from. Then go ahead and use the space below to do your own Pain/Gain flip.

ACTIVITY:
DOING THE FLIP

PART 1: YOUR POSITIVES, BENEFITS, ASPIRATIONAL BULLETS:

1. _____
2. _____
3. _____

PART 2: NOW DESCRIBE WHAT HAPPENS WHEN THOSE ARE ABSENT?

1. _____
2. _____
3. _____

PART 3: DO THE FLIP, AND MAKE THE NEGATIVE CONDITIONS GO AWAY:

1. _____
2. _____
3. _____

Feel free to do this activity with MORE than three of your marketing bullets. If you get to 7, 10, or even 15, you will have the beginnings of a powerful arsenal of sales language to use with your prospects!

Your "Indisputable Points of Proof"

This one is easy. It's like fact-checking radar for your marketing. We too often take our background, expertise, and experiences for granted, but these can be the source of our most powerful and persuasive marketing ammunition.

Your "indisputable points of proof" are concrete, tangible facts about you and your business that make a difference to your prospect's level of trust and confidence that you can deliver the goods.

Here are some examples from a variety of business owners, entrepreneurs, and independent professionals I've worked with over the years:

- ✱ Started a business at the age of 14
- ✱ Personally visited over 2,000 hospitals, clinics, and medical offices
- ✱ Addressed over 100,000 people in the course of delivering 900 seminars over the past 15 years
- ✱ *Atlanta Business Journal* 40 Under 40 winner in 2013
- ✱ Named among 25 hot speakers by the National Speakers Association
- ✱ Owned and operated Houston's largest advertising agency and grew revenues from $2 million to $40 million in six years
- ✱ Interviewed over 50 CEOs and Presidents of technology services firms
- ✱ 30 years of experience as a financial advisor and creator of the "Small Cap Business" series of books and audio programs

Whatever you can tangibly prove—use it! It counts. As long as it builds credibility and trust and RELEVANCE (direct or indirect) to your Thought Leadership Platform, people need to know about it. You should NOT be shy in sharing your accomplishments, track record, awards, firsthand experiences, and achievements.

Your Goals (Clients, Projects, Revenue, Profit)

This one is simple. Based on the monthly revenue you need and want to generate, it's time to set some goals. These can be in terms of clients, projects, revenue, profit—anything you can track that has meaningful impact on your bank account.

As an example, I'll share mine with you:

David's goals:

1. Work with minimum of five entrepreneurs and executives as one-on-one clients in concurrent rotation
2. Four paid speaking engagements for corporate and association groups per month
3. Six group programs with full enrollment (20 people) every 12 months

ACTIVITY:
YOUR SPECIFIC GOALS

1. _____
2. _____
3. _____
4. _____
5. _____

Your Strategies (What You Are Committed to Doing)

Think about the kinds of marketing activities you find easy, effortless, and enjoyable. If you like to write, use writing strategies. If you love to talk, use talking strategies. If you love technology, use technology strategies. This isn't rocket science. Let your mind go play and see what comes back!

Jot 'em down here, and we'll pick up this thread later in the 21-day program:

ACTIVITY:
YOUR FAVORITE STRATEGIES

1. _____
2. _____
3. _____
4. _____
5. _____

Your Tactics (How? When? Frequency? Who Does Them?)

Once you've got some good raw material, start thinking about what a marketing calendar might look like. From the strategies you just jotted down, how will you deploy actions around each? What will you tackle daily versus weekly versus monthly versus quarterly? How much will you delegate or outsource to others?

NOTES AND PRELIMINARY TACTICAL PLANS:

Daily, I will . . .

_____

_____

Weekly, I will . . .

_____

_____

Monthly, I will . . .

_____

_____

Quarterly, I will . . .

_____

_____

Resources, people, partners I'd like to leverage to make these happen are (webmaster, graphic designer, virtual assistant, etc.):

1. _____
2. _____
3. _____
4. _____
5. _____.

The tactical marketing tasks I have interest/availability to do myself are:

1. _____
2. _____
3. _____
4. _____
5. _____.

That's it. Whew!

YOUR 21-DAY MARKETING LAUNCH PLAN

You're doing a great job laying the foundation for ALL your marketing and business growth activities. This is important, and it will pay you back many times over for the investment you're making now of your time, energy, and thought.

Have a frosty beverage on me tonight to celebrate your good work today!

DAY 5:
PERSONAL BRANDING, DOMAIN, AND WEB SETUP

Buy your name as a domain from http://www.GoDaddy.com. If your name is not available, try buying it with your middle initial included. Even if your company is well established with its own website, YOU need a website for your own personal branding purposes as the face and voice of your business. YOU are the expert, not your faceless company.

Also, make sure to get an e-mail account with your domain, and spend some time setting it up today so that you can start communicating with the world as yourname@yourname.com.

Frankly, nothing reeks of amateur more than an e-mail address that ends in @aol.com or @comcast.net, especially when domains and e-mail accounts are less than $10 a year! It's fine to have a personal e-mail account AND a business e-mail account. But don't reach out to prospects and partners and have their first impression be, "Wow, this person doesn't even have a business e-mail address. Yikes!"

If you're interested in rebranding an existing business or branding something more than a solopreneur business model (remember your business model decisions from Day 1), you may find my Instant Branding Toolkit blog post of great interest: **http://bit.ly/instantbrand.**

Spend about an hour brainstorming the PRIMARY brand message (and web domain) you want your Thought Leadership Platform tied to. Make some decisions. When it comes to domain names, they're cheap and easy to buy. Grab all the ones that make sense for you—the names of your programs, products, services, your sound bites, your tag lines, your catch phrases, etc.

For example, even though I run my business all under the brand of Do It! Marketing, I own the domains for:

- ✸ http://www.MarketingLanguageBank.com (the phrase)
- ✸ http://www.SimpleMarketingSuccess.com (the 10-week group coaching program)
- ✸ http://www.DavidNewman.com (for speaking engagements)
- ✸ http://www.TeleseminarsForProfit.com (product)
- ✸ http://www.doitmarketingbook.com (book)
- ✸ And about 260 others

Some are active standalone websites, and some point to subpages of www.doitmarketing.com, and still others are domains that I wanted to buy simply to reserve that intellectual property on the Internet for possible later use. I might never use them, but the point is that I'd hate to have someone ELSE grab those domains because they're part of MY Thought Leadership Platform!

Oh, by the way, I also own the domain name for http://ThoughtLeadershipPlatform.com. I invented that phrase and talk about it a lot, so I want to "own" that term on the web even though I'm not currently doing anything with it.

Your Website

Now, on to your web site. If you're just starting out, you need one. And if you're running an already established business, you might consider building a new minisite dedicated to your service, product, program, niche, or market.

For example, although my main website is **http://www.doitmarketing.com**, I also own **http://www.DavidNewman.com**, which is where I direct all my speaking prospects and clients. In my case, it's just a redirect to the "Speaking" page on my main site. I do it this way because it fits my business model. (See how this all comes together?)

As another example, a few years ago, I wanted to focus on community banks as a target market for a specific set of projects, programs, and seminars. So I built a separate website for that, which you can still see (although it's no longer actively promoted): http://www.ResultsBasedBanking.com.

In both these examples, I worked with a professional web designer. And that may be a good option for you, too, if you have the financial resources to dedicate to it. It's definitely money well spent. (If you want to tap into my web team, drop me an e-mail at david@doitmarketing.com.)

For the sake of this 21-day launch, we'll assume that money is tight so you can definitely get started with a simple, do-it-yourself website.

Let's get you going. Spend some time on these four websites to learn about the easiest, fastest way to build your own website without the need for a webmaster or a resident geek to help you:

* http://www.wordpress.com/
* http://www.typepad.com
* http://www.squarespace.com/
* http://www.tumblr.com

Spend about 20 minutes on each site. Then, based on whichever platform looks the easiest and most compatible with your technical skills (if yours are ZERO, I recommend TypePad!), open an account and spend 45 minutes experimenting with the features, layouts, and options for posting your web pages.

Expect to spend between two and three hours total on today's tasks. Good work this week! You ROCK!

DAY 6:
RESEARCH AND (RE-)SET YOUR PRICES

Research some industry websites and directories of companies like yours. Locate the prices and price ranges of six to eight competing firms and professionals in your field, and take note of minimum and maximum price points.

If this information is hard to find for your business, you may need to enlist a friend to do some secret shopping on your behalf to collect pricing, proposals, and fee information from local, regional, and national competitors.

If you're just starting out, decide on a pricing "anchor" so that you have a firm number to quote for your various products, services, and offerings once you're in marketing and sales conversations.

If you're an experienced business owner, consider this: You have monthly revenue goals, right? Once you hit your goals consistently at your CURRENT pricing levels for SIX CONSECUTIVE MONTHS, it is time to raise your prices.

Yes, really!

Too many business owners stay stuck for YEARS at price points that are too low. They talk with their entrepreneur pals and realize that those OTHER businesses are making 20–50 percent more money, and they wonder why.

- ✴ Entrepreneur A: "Well, back in 2005, I thought our prices were the same."
- ✴ Entrepreneur B: "Back in 2005, they were!"
- ✴ Entrepreneur A: "So what happened?"
- ✴ Entrepreneur B: "I listened to David Newman. [OK. I made that part up!] Over the years, whenever we hit our goals for six months straight, I raised prices between 5 and 10 percent. Repeat clients either didn't notice or didn't mind and were happy to go upstream with us. New clients didn't know the difference."

Today is the day to decide whether you'd rather be Entrepreneur A or Entrepreneur B.

DAY 7:
ARTICLE DAY

No new marketing tasks for today. Instead, you get to focus 100 percent of your energy on brainstorming a collection of article ideas and writing two or three articles. These will become an important part of your Thought Leadership Platform and ongoing marketing arsenal.

Brainstorming Article Topics and Titles

Start by sitting down with a clean sheet of paper. Using the following article idea starters, jot down three to five potential topics or titles in each category based on your topic expertise and based on some of the good work you've already done as you've been working your way through this book.

Remember that your articles should focus on addressing your buyer persona's most common challenges, problems, and gaps. What are their personal and professional heartaches and headaches that they want answers to? In which areas are they hungry for strategies and tactics?

Here are some tried-and-true article title formulas you can use and adapt for your first batch of articles.

1. How to ...
2. Five strategies ...
3. Three keys to ...
4. The number one problem with ... and how to solve it
5. Unlocking your ...
6. The three biggest traps in [topic] and how to avoid them
7. Ten tips for ...
8. Everything you know about [topic] is wrong

ACTIVITY:
YOUR ARTICLE TITLE IDEAS

1. _____
2. _____
3. _____
4. _____
5. _____

Article Writing

Aim for 400- to 600-word articles. These are short enough to capture your prospects' attention but long enough to make one main point and demonstrate your expertise with three to five supporting short tips, ideas, and pointers.

If you're like most business owners, entrepreneurs, and independent professionals, the hardest part of the article-writing process is actually sitting down and starting. So I'm here to support you.

SIT DOWN!
START!!
There. Good job. Congratulations on completing today's assignment.

DAY 8:
REST DAY

Stop. Rest. Relax. Today is a "white space" day so that you can celebrate your progress thus far. Have you been dying to goof off? Play hooky? See a movie? Take the dog for a long nature walk? Give yourself a mini-spa day? Eat pizza, chocolate, and ice cream in front of the TV?

Today is the day to DO IT!

Enjoy!

DAY 9:
WEBSITE SETUP OR REVIEW/REVISION

If you're just starting—or restarting—your business, we're going to focus a lot of time, energy, and love on building your blog-based website using the easy-to-manage blog platform you chose for yourself on Day 5.

If you're an established business, you might not need to build anything new. Today will be focused on revisiting and revising your website so that it's the best possible articulation of your fabulousness!

For the sake of this assignment, I'll assume you're building your web presence simply because my instructions are more detailed for the initial build, but you can use these ideas for revising, too.

Here's the ingredient list for a credible website for any business owner, entrepreneur, or independent professional:

- ✹ **About:** Information about your credentials and experience
- ✹ **Contact:** E-mail, phone, fax, physical street address
- ✹ **Services/products:** A list of your available services, products, programs, types of projects
- ✹ **Resources/articles:** Published articles, tip sheets, tools, downloads, videos, audios, and other valuable content

- ❋ **News/blog**
- ❋ **Service/product:** Personally, I like to have an individual landing page for each service I'm promoting so I can give more detail to prospective clients and provide more information. You could also just include descriptions on your main Service/Product pages to simplify things for now.
- ❋ **Clients/customers/sample projects:** A listing of past and present clients/ projects if they'll lend additional credibility to your work. (You may wish to include short testimonial blurbs on every page of your site)

DAY 10:
BUILDING INBOUND LINKS

If you've been following along in real time, your basic website is ready for prime time. And if your site was already up and running, it's time to promote it more systematically than you might have before.

The goal today is simple: Let your existing network know about your (new or revised) website. These are the places where you've already spent time getting to know colleagues and members of your target market. Unfortunately, these networks won't lead to new business if no one knows exactly what you offer. It's time to help them find out!

You have one easy exercise today. You're going to add the link to your professional website to at least 10 existing networking sites.

Here are some examples to get you started:

- ❋ Forum signatures (Don't spam forums by starting threads or making posts just to link to your site)
- ❋ Comments you leave on relevant industry, topic, or professional blogs in your field
- ❋ Your social networking profiles (LinkedIn, Facebook, YouTube, Pinterest, and/or additional professional and industry networks)
- ❋ LinkedIn Group posts relevant to your expertise when you leave a content-rich answer to someone else's question
- ❋ Amazon.com book reviews OR creating your own Listmania lists or "So You Want to" guides
- ❋ Your Twitter account (Announce that your new site was just launched, and link to it promoting one of your free resources)

Today's tasks should be easy and fun.

Spend up to three hours researching the best places to leave your mark and then building these links on those sites with some value-rich contributions. Even a short note, comment, book list, or suggestion has value. (Remember: no spamming or thinly disguised sales pitches!)

Nice job today.

DAY 11:
ASSEMBLING YOUR BASIC PRESENTATION

Today you will build a 20- to 25-slide PowerPoint or Keynote deck to flesh out your first (or NEXT) client-magnet presentation that will position you as an expert in your field.

Note: This is a tremendously useful exercise whether or not you actually plan to use software like PowerPoint as a presentation support tool while speaking.

Think in terms of each slide representing a self-contained "chapter," which might consist of:

* A key philosophy of yours
* A little known fact or tip that benefits your target market
* One of your customer success stories
* A metaphor or analogy that makes a key point
* A startling or little known statistic and its implications
* One of the planks of your thought leadership platform

Tip: Do NOT think in terms of putting bullets on slides. (You can add text or notes for yourself in the Notes area below each slide.) Think in terms of putting CONCEPTS, IDEAS, and VISUALS on each slide.

Today's task should take you between two and three hours, AND, if you're doing it right, it will be fun, engaging, and absorbing.

Have a great day and do have FUN with it.

To make this process easy and effective, grab a free digital copy of Seth Godin's *Really Bad PowerPoint,* and apply all the principles he outlines to YOUR presentation. Download your free copy now at http://bit.ly/sethppt

DAY 12:
BUILD A SIMPLE SPEAKER ONE-SHEET

Now that your flagship presentation has some texture and shape, you can summarize it on a speaker one-sheet. Local networking groups, chambers of commerce, and association chapters often want to see this before booking you to speak in front of your hand-selected target market of prospects. Lay out a simple one-sheet in Microsoft Word, or pay a little extra for a designer to format it more professionally.

The building blocks are:

1. One or more Topics/Programs
2. Target Audience(s)
3. Benefits (especially in headlines and program titles)
4. Your Mini-Biography
5. Your Sample Client List
6. Testimonial clips about the quality of your programs
7. Your Contact Information

DAY 13:
FIND SPEAKING LEADS AND PLACES TO DELIVER YOUR CLIENT-MAGNET PRESENTATION

Refer back to Chapters 25 and 26 in this book to identify, target, and connect with audiences of your high-probability prospects. These groups can be local, regional, and national in scope. They can be in your backyard or, depending on your business and your specific prospects, they may be well worth a cross-country plane trip.

DAY 14:
ASK FOR AIR (ADVICE, INSIGHTS, RECOMMENDATIONS)

You've done a lot of good work, and you should now reach out to your team of advocates, allies, friends, colleagues, and others who know you and love you.

Tell them what you're up to, whom you've decided to serve, and whom you'd like to meet or be introduced to. Also share with them the types of networking groups and associations you'd like to do a presentation for.

Then, as my friend, networking and referral marketing expert Michael Goldberg, recommends, ask them for their advice, insights, and recommendations (A-I-R). This is where your initial networking and referral marketing strategy will kick in. As you meet new decision-makers and influencers, you will continue building your web of connections.

DAY 15:
ARTICLE SUBMISSION DAY

At this point, you should have two or three articles written and ready to go from your efforts on Day 7. Now it's time to offer them to relevant publications, trade and professional magazines, websites, and associations of your target market.

ACTIVITY:
YOUR ARTICLE SUBMISSION TEMPLATE

Send a simple e-mail that follows this exact template:

Dear Bob,

I'm writing to submit several articles for your consideration for [publication].

They are attached below.

If one or more of these would be useful for you, please feel free to use them as your editorial needs dictate. Simply drop me an e-mail when you decide to use one.

If you'd like me to submit an article specially written on a subject of your choice, please don't hesitate to get in touch.

Sincerely,

[YOU]

[e-mail] [phone]

[website URL]

Submit e-mails like this to at least 20 different publications that serve your target market, industry, and/or buyer persona.

If you contact state and national associations and niche industry publications dedicated to your audience, topic, or field, you WILL get your article published, and you WILL establish relationships with the editors and publishers you reach.

Furthermore, you are now positioning yourself and your company as the go-to experts in front of the very people who have the ability to buy your products, services, and programs.

Studies have shown for years that EARNED media (articles written BY you or ABOUT you) pack approximately 20 TIMES the marketing power of PAID media (i.e., advertising).

Think about it this way: Would you rather pay $8,000 for the full-page glossy magazine ad in your industry's leading trade publication that people flip right by? OR would you rather be the industry expert who wrote the article on the facing page that your prospects will read, highlight, tear out, photocopy, and pass around the office?

I thought so. That's why, starting today, you can make article marketing a part of your ongoing new business strategy.

DAY 16:
REST DAY

* Do something you really enjoy
* Eat healthy
* Get some exercise
* Have some fun

You've been working hard, so you deserve a breather. We have five days to go, and you're doing great!

DAY 17:
PRODUCT DEVELOPMENT DAY

Many business owners, entrepreneurs, and independent professionals claim that they could get all the business they want IF ONLY they could get in front of more prospects with a face-to-face or voice-to-voice meeting.

When I ask my marketing coaching clients and seminar participants why they feel this is true, the response is often, "People don't see the value of what we do unless I spend about 20 minutes clearing up common misconceptions, sharing some valuable insights and ideas, and answering their questions."

As soon as I respond that this process can be automated and scaled way, way UP with a simple information product, most business owners' faces light up with the revenue-generating potential of this idea.

The simplest and fastest product to create is a 30-minute audio program of your best insights and advice that you would deliver to an interested prospect face-to-face.

Because you've already created your flagship presentation, we'll focus on creating your first product as an audio.

ACTIVITY:
CREATING YOUR AUDIO

Based on your best ideas and most valuable tips, you're ready to capture a smooth and well-practiced audio, either in a pocket digital recorder or directly into your PC or Mac using a quality USB microphone. The advantage to using your PC or Mac and a good microphone is that you'll be able to use the best free digital recording and editing software—Audacity—to make your recording sound professional. Once your recording is finished, use Audacity to edit out any ums, ahs, goofs, coughs, and retakes. Then save your final edited digital audio. (Download and try out Audacity here: http://audacity.sourceforge.net/)

To complete your product package, have your audio transcribed. You can find reliable, affordable transcription services on sites like Elance.com, Guru.com, and Odesk.com.

Have some fun with your product development day, and don't forget to put lots of YOUR personality into your recording. After all, as a professional expert, THAT is your secret sauce!

PS: Feel stuck? Use the raw material you developed in Chapters 12–16 as a starting point for your script.

DAY 18:
CREATE YOUR E-MAIL AND LIST-BUILDING PLATFORM

Once you have something to say—and sell—your next task will be to set up an account on Constant Contact.

Here is a special link, which will give you a FREE 30-day trial plus special bonuses if you decide to sign up: **http://bit.ly/constantcontactfree.**

ACTIVITY:
SMART E-MAIL MARKETING

Once you've gotten your Constant Contact account up and running, place a Join My Mailing List box on the home page of your blog-based website that you set up on Day 5. This box enables you to capture e-mail addresses from your website.

Customize the box with different styles to best match your website. Styles include forms, button, and text links, all in a variety of colors and fonts. Constant Contact makes this process very simple and user-friendly.

Next, import your initial contacts from your existing e-mail software (Outlook, Outlook Express, Gmail, Yahoo Mail, etc.), your contact manager (Act!), or your sales automation database (Salesforce.com, QuickBooks), depending on what you use.

Make sure to segment your contacts into different lists for maximum effectiveness. For example, create three separate lists: one for your distributors, one for your customers, and one for people who opt in to your website.

Sometimes you'll want to send a blast to everyone, but there will be MORE times when you'll want to laser-focus your e-blasts to only certain segments of your list with a specific purpose.

Once you've made these decisions and done the basic subscriber list setup, you're ready to capture e-mail addresses on your website and build your base of fans and followers.

Over time, you'll send them news, updates, tips, valuable free resources, special offers, and subscriber-only deals on your programs, products, and services. Design each e-mail blast with one simple guideline in mind: Make your information too good to throw away so that your subscribers look forward to reading each update from you!

DAY 19:
SOCIAL MEDIA DAY

Today you'll set up (or re-engage with) your social media accounts. We'll focus on the four most important ones to get you going.

ACTIVITY:
SETTING UP SOCIAL MEDIA ACCOUNTS

Set up accounts and spend some time getting familiar with:

- LinkedIn
- Facebook
- YouTube
- Twitter

For excellent self-study resources on each of these, I've prepared some links for you to get you up and running fast. Read these four articles today by visiting www.doitmarketing.com/book.

- "33 Ways to Use LinkedIn for Business"
- "32 Ways to Use Facebook for Business"
- "YouTube for Your Business"
- "How to Use Twitter to Grow Your Business"

DAY 20:
MAP OUT YOUR ORGANIZATION CHART

At last count, the U.S. Census bureau reported that there are 27,757,676 small businesses in the country and that 21,708,021 of those firms are nonemployer firms, meaning that they are a company of ONE: the owner. (Source: http://www.census.gov/econ/smallbus.html.)

Based on those numbers, it's clear that some small businesses have employees but that most (over 75 percent) do not.

At the same time, very few SUCCESSFUL solo business owners run their business ALONE.

They bring in help: interns, part-time folks, professional advisors, and outsourcing partners.

Today—to continue the theme of taking your business SERIOUSLY—you will map out your virtual organization, including your board of advisors and the roles and positions that you may be filling externally, internally, or part-time.

ACTIVITY:
YOUR ORG CHART OF THE FUTURE

At the top of the organization chart is the box for YOU; you're the CEO.

Then start to fill in the roles and functions (not specific people yet) that you would LIKE to have on your team. STRETCH yourself here.

IMAGINE that money is no object—that you've just won the lottery!

Don't worry about WHERE to find these people. Don't worry about WHAT to pay them. Don't worry about HOW you'd keep them all busy.

Wave a magic wand and put yourself at the head of a multimillion-dollar business, and let's figure out who would be on THAT team.

Here are some starter ideas for you:

* Accountant/bookkeeper
* Attorney/legal
* Marketing manager/salesperson
* Administrative assistant
* Product development manager

- ✹ Technology guru/webmaster
- ✹ Intern(s)—one or more dedicated to specific tasks
- ✹ Writer/ghostwriter/blog manager
- ✹ Public relations/media manager
- ✹ Researcher
- ✹ Board of advisors: Include allies, advocates, long-time clients, entrepreneur buddies, corporate friends, and the like

Once you have all these slots organized on a single piece of paper (or even better—on a flipchart with colorful markers), it's time to think some more...

BUT WAIT!

Before you do anything else, consider something that I've found to be 100 percent true in running my OWN business and helping hundreds of other entrepreneurs and executives: **YOU can't get any place other than where you are right now.**

What does THAT mean? If you're running a $100,000 business and you want to get to $500,000, you need to start thinking and acting like the owner of a $500,000 business TODAY.

If you're already running a $500,000 business today and you want to get to $2 million—you guessed it—you have to start acting like the CEO of your $2 million business. Right now—TODAY!

So make THOSE decisions.

Find and HIRE those people.

Pursue and land THOSE clients and contracts.

Don't wait. Don't hold off until you get more credentials, more business experience, more confidence. ACT AS IF right now. Otherwise, you'll stay right where you are. I'm not saying that's bad. I'm just saying it's true based on everything I've seen, experienced, and worked on for other successful entrepreneurs.

DAY 21:
YOU MADE IT!

Congratulations! Your first 21 days of work have been action-packed and intense.

Now the question becomes, "How do you sustain and build your momentum?"

If you started this program with nothing, you've made AMAZING progress.

If you started this program as an already established business owner or entrepreneur, you've made some tweaks, changes, and adjustments to further sharpen your Thought Leadership Platform AND your marketing tools. Awesome!!

Here's the rub: Whether you've been doing this for 21 days or 21 years, now your challenge is to stay hungry and NOT to get arrogant or complacent. The key is the mantra, "Start with zero every day." Consider doing this exercise each morning.

ACTIVITY:
START WITH ZERO EVERY DAY

Pretend it's your first day in business. You have no track record. You have no baggage. You have no clients, no customers, no labels, no brand, no nuthin'.
What would you do?

Measurements and metrics to begin tracking TODAY (revenue, clients, hours, projects, profits, etc.):

_____

_____

Projects to start TODAY:

_____

_____

Allies or colleagues to contact TODAY:

_____

_____

Goals and targets for TODAY:

_____

_____

YOUR 21-DAY DO IT! MARKETING PLAYBOOK

After your 21-day Launch Plan, you can begin to work on your 21-Day Do It! Marketing Playbook. **This will serve as your perpetual marketing plan that you can use every single day.**

Your 21-Day DO IT! Marketing Playbook, templates, and tools are available online right now at **http://www.doitmarketing.com/book.**

Don't wait another moment. Download it, fill it out, and start your daily progress toward getting MORE leads, BETTER prospects, and BIGGER sales. Whether you implement your playbook strategies on your own, with a Certified Do It! Marketing Coach, or with an accountability partner, they are designed to give you the structure, tools, and focused guidance you need to approach your marketing tasks in a whole new way.

The bottom line is that now you're on your own. It's up to YOU:

* To earn your keep every day
* To deliver the goods every day
* To put fresh targets on your radar daily

If I can be of service to you in the future, PLEASE don't hesitate to contact me.

Furthermore, I INSIST that you call or e-mail me to celebrate your success stories. Whether that's next week, next month, or next year, I'd love to hear from you about a specific tool, strategy, or idea that you RAN with and that worked brilliantly for you and your business.

And of course, YOU get all the credit because you made the leap from IDEAS into ACTION . . . and **only action creates results!**

Be well. I'm watching you.

All the best,

David

E-mail: David@doitmarketing.com

Tel: (610) 716-5984

ACKNOWLEDGMENTS

The first acknowledgement has to go to YOU—for buying this book, for reading it, and for applying its strategies, tactics, and tools to grow your business.

After you, it gets harder to count all the individuals, friends, clients, collaborators, mentors, trusted advisors, and supporters who have made this book—and all the rest of my work—so easy, effortless, and enjoyable. Unlike some authors who don't even try, here goes.

First I'd like to thank my parents for not having a stroke when I announced I was leaving the pre-med program at Franklin & Marshall College to pursue a career in the theater. **Thank you to Dr. Gordon Wickstrom,** who modeled the highest gift of catalyzing the best in others while making them feel personally important and professionally capable. What do you get when you cross healing with drama? Of course, you get marketing.

My amazing partner, Vanessa Christman, gets a ton of credit for sticking with her lunatic husband through thick (my waistline) and thin (my hairline). Without you, none of this would be any fun at all. Truly.

My two awesome kids, Becca and Charlie, Woofie the Wonder Dog, and Mimi the cat also went to heroic lengths to put up with me long before, during, and after the writing of this book. I love you guys like bananas.

Professionally, the list is even longer. Big thanks to my book agent, Michael Snell. He does business the old-fashioned way, and it works amazingly well for all concerned. I'm grateful to my pal Gene Marks for sharing Mike's genius with me. At AMACOM, Ellen Kadin is a rock star. She knows what works, and she makes sure I DO IT! Her steady dedication to our shared vision of a business book with attitude shows up on every page. Big thanks and kudos to the AMACOM design team for realizing that vision with the bold design of this book.

And for you aspiring or experienced authors—especially those of

261

you who, like me, hate to be edited—meet my editor extraordinaire, Christopher Murray. Chris "got" this book right from the start and was an amazing collaborator, organizer, and advocate for the business-building ideas I wanted to share with you. Find Chris online at www.ChrisMurrayEditor. com, and put your project in the hands of a supremely insightful editor and the best friend your writing ever had.

I deeply thank Dr. Michael Ray of Stanford Business School for introducing me to the Creativity in Business MBA course that changed my life. The very best advice he gave me was, "Stop starting things and get more into doing." The DNA of Michael's wisdom runs throughout my work, my life, and, by extension, this book.

Thank you to my pals from my corporate days: Sandy Frick, Trish Koons, Neal Duffy, Kim Nuzzaci, and Benjamin Laden, who were crazy enough to hire me, work with me, and recruit me away from one job into the next for a great 10-year run. I don't know what you were thinking, but I'm grateful for all the fun we had working for the man.

Thank you to four very special people who helped me at every point in my entrepreneurial journey, including the good, the bad, and the ugly: in mind (Terry Fisher), in body (Nick Odorisio), in spirit (Scott Simons), and in career (Ford R. Myers).

My involvement in the National Speakers Association (NSA) and Canadian Association of Professional Speakers (CAPS) has been an invaluable source of inspiration, insights, and friendships. Thank you to my mentors, role models, and friends: Laurie Brown, Gideon Grunfeld, Michael Roby, Kirstin Carey, Steve Coscia, Avish Parashar, Michael Goldberg, Todd Cohen, Brian Walter, John Reddish, Marvin LeBlanc, Carol Fredrickson, Tom Stoyan, Toni Newman, Brian Lee, Scott McKain, Alan Zimmerman, Frank Bucaro, LeAnn Thieman, Thom Winninger, Patricia Fripp, Alan Weiss, Bob Burg, John Jantsch, David Meerman Scott, Brian Tracy, Randy Gage, and Jeffrey Gitomer.

Thank you to my speaker bureau partners and friends: Andrea Gold, Shawn Ellis, Katrina Mitchell, and Nancy Vogl. You are the sharpest, most dedicated folks in the business, and you model excellence and integrity in everything you do.

Thank you to my expert contributors: Jay Baer, Scott Ginsberg, Corey Perlman, Dan Janal, Mark LeBlanc, Barry Moltz, Mark Hunter, Henry DeVries,

Tom Searcy, Melinda Emerson, Stephanie Chandler, Mary Foley, Gene Marks, and Viveka Von Rosen. You are each superheroes in your own realm, and I hugely appreciate your generosity of expertise.

Thank you to my colleagues in Vistage International, the world's largest CEO peer group organization: Jose Palomino, Gerry Lantz, Chris Farias, Scott Messer, Brian Carney, Skip Lange, Carl Francis, Marcia O'Connor, Michael Gidlewski, Steve Van Valin, and Jim Lucas. You've shared your insights and advice with me even when I didn't want to hear it, didn't follow it, and didn't want to believe it. However, you were right four times out of five. I'm learning.

Thank you to my Do It! Marketing team members, past and present. Especially the über awesome Catherine Bernard, the ultra-amazing Katie Hanna, the super-productive Rachel Rodden, and Liz Crider, aka "the team member who got away." I love working with you and appreciate you more than you know.

Thank you to my amazing clients. Man, when YOU work, this program works! I'm continually humbled and grateful for your confidence, your business, your friendship, and the credit that you bring to our work by DOING IT consistently, smartly, and bravely. You are the embodiment of my mantra, "Only action creates results." Thank you for the privilege of working alongside you as you create your next level of success.

Thank you for reading. I appreciate you.

INDEX

ABOUT THE AUTHOR

David Newman is a nationally acclaimed marketing speaker who presents to groups of entrepreneurs and executives who want to generate MORE leads, BETTER prospects, and BIGGER sales.

David has been working at the intersection of marketing, technology, and professional services since 1992. His past clients include Accenture, KPMG, Oracle, IBM, Microsoft, PriceWaterhouseCoopers, and 44 of the Fortune 500.

He is an experienced professional services marketer, professional speaker, and strategic business coach. David has presented to over 600 groups, including state and national associations, nonprofit organizations, and companies of every size.

David's career as a corporate insider included stints at a boutique technology consulting firm in Delaware, the prestigious Professional Development Institute at management consulting powerhouse Towers Perrin, and Global Professional Services for PeopleSoft (back when they were ranked sixth on *Fortune*'s list of 100 Best Places to Work in America).

David has been featured and quoted in *The New York Times, Investors Business Daily, FastCompany.com, Sales & Marketing Management, Selling Power, Business 2.0, Business2Business, NBC-TV*, and *Entrepreneur* magazine.

David is married to the number one most amazing woman on the planet, has two great kids, and has the world's sweetest Labrador retriever named Woofie (visit www.whereswoofie.com). **FREE** marketing resources, templates, and tools are waiting for you online at **www.doitmarketing.com/book.**